Ministering Freedom
to the Sexually Broken

Ministering Freedom
to the Sexually Broken

Doris M. Wagner,
General Editor

WAGNER
PUBLICATIONS

Ministering Freedom to the Sexually Broken
Copyright © 2003 by Doris M. Wagner
ISBN 1-58502-038-9
Library of Congress Control Number: 2003108601

Published by
Wagner Publications
11005 N. Highway 83
Colorado Springs, CO 80921
www.wagnerpublications.org

Cover design by
Imagestudios
100 East St. Suite 105
Colorado Springs, CO 80903
719-578-0351   www.imagestudios.net

Edit and interior design by Rebecca Sytsema

Rights for publishing this book in other languages are contracted by Gospel Literature International (GLINT). GLINT also provides technical help for the adaptation, translation, and publishing of Bible study resources and books in scores of languages worldwide. For further information, contact GLINT, P.O. Box 4060, Ontario, CA 91761-1003, USA. You may also send e-mail to glintint@aol.com, or visit their web site at www.glint.org.

1   2   3   4   5   6   7   8   9   09   08   07   06   05   04   03

Contents

Meet the Contributors

While most Christians believe that demons exist somewhere in the world, a relatively small number of Christians realize that demons can affect their daily lives; and even fewer know how to effectively deal with one. But that is changing! Over the past few decades there has been a great resurgence in both the understanding and practice of deliverance. Because there is a need to understand this type of ministry, I decided to offer a useful series of books to help both the local church and the average Christian be equipped to effectively minister freedom from demonic oppression. Each book in the series will deal with a specific topic.

In this third book of the series, I have gathered experts in the field of deliverance to the sexually broken who can help us understand the complex issues of human sexuality and how the enemy can take advantage of both sin and victimization to bring sexual bondage. They will also offer practical advice for ministering deliverance in this area. I'd like to briefly introduce each of them to you:

Doris M. Wagner

The Lord has used me to help many people find free-dom from sexual bondages over the past 20 years. In my chapter, I address many hard-to-discuss issues head on which often plague victims of lust and show how those who have been caught in sexual bondage can gently be lead back to wholeness through deliverance and inner healing prayer.

Peter Horrobin

Peter is the author of *Healing Through Deliverance, Vols. I* and *II*, which are some of the most treasured books in my library. An excellent and entertaining speaker and writer, Peter has masterfully dealt with the issue of sexual sin in Chapter Two of this book, and the important topic of soul ties in Chapter Three. It is, without a doubt, the best treatment of the topic I have ever seen.

Tim and Anne Evans

Tim and Anne are close friends and inde-fatigable youth workers. They have labored for years to help young people find Christ and get discipled in the Christian walk, including helping them understand a biblical view of sexuality. In their chapter, they give an honest view of what teens and college-age people are facing in a society bombarded with sexual images and expectations.

John Eckhardt

John is a good friend and collegue who has labored for the Lord in innercity Chicago. The Lord led John and his congregation into an effective deliverance ministry that has blessed the lives of countless people. In his ministry, John has come face to face with the cruel aftermath of abortion. In his chapter, he shares his highly valuable and useful insights on the topic.

David Kyle Foster

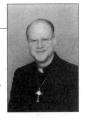

David has successfully left a homosexual lifestyle in the Hollywood scene, and thoroughly understands the struggles of others doing so. He shares the story of his pilgrimage frequently as part of his ministry. Now an Episcopal priest, David is serving the Lord very effectively and helping others become free from homosexual bondages. His chapter is an excellent and needful contribution to this book.

Tom R. Hawkins

Tom has experience in a difficult and complex field—Dissociative Identity Disorder (formerly called Multiple Personality Disorder). Those suffering from this disorder are generally victims of extreme, prolonged trauma, often including sexual abuse as children. You will learn much from Tom's scholarly and personal treatment of this often misunderstood issue.

Chapter One

Ministering to Those in Sexual Bondage

Doris M. Wagner

Doris Wagner along with her husband, C. Peter Wagner, founded Global Harvest Ministries in 1992, with a vision of bringing together prayer networks for the purpose of focusing their collective prayer power on world evangelism. Doris serves in Global Harvest Ministries as the CEO. A deliverance minister for 20 years, she has helped set countless people free from various addictions and bondages. Because of her desire to see mobilization for deliverance within the church, she now specializes in deliverance training, speaking at regional and national conferences, and has taught practical seminars in many nations of the world. Her books and teaching resources are available by calling 888-563-5150, or at www.arsenalbooks.com.

God created human beings with the capability of reproduction. In the very first chapter of the Bible, Scripture states "So God created man in His own image; in the image of God He created him; male and female He created them. Then God blessed them, and God said to them, 'Be fruitful and multiply; fill the earth and subdue it'" (Gen. 1:27-28).

In Chapter 2, we find a detailed description of the creation of man and his wife. God "brought her to the man" (v. 22), and Scripture then says in verse 24, "Therefore a man shall leave his father and mother and be joined to his wife, and they shall become one flesh." Apparently, God Himself had set up the marriage institution because He made Eve to be Adam's wife and gave instructions for future men and their wives. They were to start their own homes and "become one."

Becoming One

"Becoming one" speaks to me of an inseparable union. Note that Eve was created for two specific reasons, as noted in Genesis 2:18. First, "It is not good that man should be alone" and second, "I will make him a helper comparable to him." This speaks to me about God's interest in the emotional side of Adam; and apparently companionship, love, caring, friendship, and the like were needed by Adam. It also speaks to me about the practical issues to be handled in life: that having a comparable helper alongside the man was what God intended in order for the job to be complete.

Just as an aside, I have always smiled as I have read the account of creation and particularly God's last act of creation: the making of the woman. Note that as God created things one by one, the phrase appears "And God saw that it was good." Then, as mentioned above, God saw that one thing in all of creation was "not good" and that was "that man should be alone" (Gen. 2:18). There was still one thing lacking, and that was the creation of woman to become "the other half of man," as it were. Once she was created and they became "one," the job was apparently finished and "God saw everything that He had made, and indeed it was *very good*" (Gen. 2:18, emphasis added). It took the making of the woman to bring creation to a higher level than it had been previously.

The Enemy and the Curse

But Satan enters the picture in Chapter 3. As the angel who wanted glory and worship for himself, he approached Eve and twisted the command and will of God from something good to something bad. Things went downhill fast. Satan was cursed (Gen. 3: 14-15); the husband would rule over the wife and she would bring forth children with pain; the ground was cursed and man would have to work hard to make it produce crops; and they were told that they would eventually die and their bodies would decompose. Lastly, the couple was expelled from the garden.

Satan has been working to continue to twist the commands and will of God ever since that fateful event. One of the most common ways is to confuse the marriage directives of God and to deceive people into thinking that God's commands concerning sex and marriage can be called into question.

When God told Adam and Eve to "be fruitful and multiply," the idea was in order for that to happen, they had to engage in sex. Since God Himself had created their bodies, you can bet that they were beautiful and perfect – the most handsome man and gorgeous woman ever to exist. They would have had the best sexual experiences of all time. And this was one of the things that Satan set out to pervert.

Lust Enters the Picture

By Chapter 6 of Genesis, the earth was filled with corruption and violence, except for Noah and his family. So God started all over again after the flood. Many Bible scholars believe that Genesis 9:24 speaks of homosexuality initiated by Ham against his father, Noah, when he was drunk. So apparently it didn't take long for lust to enter the picture again, even though there were but a handful of people on earth.

Sex and lust have been problems ever since. The Bible certainly is not silent on these issues, for there is much instruction needed from God to keep His people on course. Sex is a very important part of life and Satan works overtime to entice, deceive, pervert, victimize, and otherwise take a God-given gift and bring confusion at best and horror at worst.

As I have been praying deliverance over people for about 20 years now, there have been very few people to come into my office who have not needed deliverance from sexual demons to some degree. In this chapter, I will deal with a few of the more common ones and some of my very good friends who work in the field of deliverance will tackle other lust issues in the rest of this book.

Pornography

Satan seems to be present when new technology is invented. He invariably goes to work attempting to pervert it to his advantage. He has had great success, particularly in the various forms of communication, as he has used them in the spread of pornography.

My *Random House Webster's College Dictionary* defines pornography as "writings, photographs, movies, etc., intended to arouse sexual excitement." Among the earliest would probably be art, both drawings and sculpture. People have tried to capture the beauty of God's creation – snow-capped mountains with blue sky, puffy clouds, and autumn colored trees. Exquisite flowers; birds and butterflies; mouthwatering fruit of many sizes, shapes and colors; a laughing child's countenance; an apple tree in full blossom or laden with perfect fruit; or a magnificent, shiny horse standing knee deep in green grass in the noonday sun would be frequent subjects of drawings or sculptures.

But somebody, one day very long ago, decided to draw some shameful pictures and make some obscene clay or marble images to sell. The word spread and many people were drawn to look at them for the excitement they elicited. It became a lucrative business, and pornography was born. It has thrived ever since.

In my experience praying for people I find that many struggle with porn. It seems to be highly addictive, producing images in the mind that won't go away, and often leaving the person with an insatiable thirst for more. As the definition above states, porn has pushed its way into books (just imagine – the first printing press was made in order to get the Bible into the hands of the common people!), magazines, photos, and movies. It has greatly proliferated through videos, DVDs, CDs, and especially the Internet. The people who run the industry have figured out how to worm their way into multitudinous sites used for shopping or research, technical sites, and the like, to link them to their well over 60,000 porn sites in hopes of displaying and selling their wares. And they are being very successful.

Opening the Door for a Demon

Why do people "struggle?" It is because repeated exposure to porn will open the door for a demon of pornography to enter and set up housekeeping. It will not just leave on its own, but must be confronted with a power that is stronger in order to evict it. Demons (evil spirits) seek human hosts, much the same as parasites, such as lice or pinworms, attach themselves to human bodies and feed off of them. But they need to find a place to attach themselves. People who do not mess with porn do not need to worry about demons of porn. There has to be exposure to lice- or pinworm-contaminated dirt in order for people to become infested. In other words: no exposure, no infestation. But in order for the lice or pinworms to be evicted, medication much stronger than they needs to be applied to rid the body of them.

As I said above, demons will not leave on their own. As a matter of fact, they can persuade their host to invite more in. Pornography frequently leads to problems such as compulsive masturbation, fornication, victimization, and others. These demons must be confronted with the authority and name of Jesus and be ordered out. This is what gets rid of the demons and decontaminates the person. It should be mentioned that reinfestation is a possibility and, in that case, the procedure will need to be administered again.

Some folks get the idea that deliverance brings immunity for life, but not so. Jesus' advice to the woman taken in adultery in John 8 holds true: "Go, and sin no more" (v. 11). Folks who have been bound by demons of pornography need to take drastic measures to totally shun it forevermore. However, I have found that persons who have been delivered from these demons are so grateful that they do not find it that difficult to overcome the temptation.

Getting Down to the Roots

How do many people get involved in lust to the degree that they become demonized? When I begin to minister to a person who suffers from demons of lust, I ask two basic questions: (1) "Do you really want me to pray for you and be free from these bondages?" Surprisingly enough, some do not. But if they are desperate for God to clean them up, when it comes to sexual issues that they have invited in, the battle is already half won. Time after time, a man or woman has come to me with tears streaming down their cheeks asking for help. This is excellent material to work with because deliverance will usually be an easy job. The demons know that they are on their way out and are trembling already.

And, (2) "Tell me about your family, and when your problems began." We find that we always need to probe into the person's history because, as Scripture says over and over again, the sins of the fathers are passed on to the children. Demons of lust have a great tendency to be inherited. What does this mean?

Let me give you an example from my experience. I frequently pray for people with a problem of compulsive masturbation. The question I ask first is "When did it begin?" One man told me – "It has been a problem as long as I can remember - I was probably around four." Now, that's unnatural! One needs to conclude that this little kid had some supernatural help.

Inherited Lust

So we probe further to see if we can glean information about his father or mother and both grandparents on both sides of the family. We ask questions such as: "Were you conceived out of wedlock?" (We find that persons conceived in lust often struggle with lust.) "Was there unfaithfulness that was a well known fact in your family?" "Did things such as pornography, adultery, child sexual abuse,

> Sex is a very important part of life and Satan works overtime to entice, deceive, pervert, victimize, and otherwise take a God-given gift and bring confusion at best and horror at worst.

prostitution, or the like find their way into your family?" If there are affirmative answers to these questions, we need to pray against a spirit of "inherited lust" for starters. That needs to be uprooted before we go on to the problems the individual has in his or her own life.

Just how do we pray against a spirit of inherited lust? I find that there is great relief to the person when I say, "Hey, this was not all your fault – you had some help getting started on this path." Well, then, who is to blame? Obviously, much blame can be placed on the person who let this sin into the family line. They made it easy for a demon of inherited lust to draw its host close to other opportunities for sexual sin. Okay, then, what do we do about it?

It is important that the person seeking deliverance from an inherited spirit of lust forgive the one who let the problem into the family line. It does not matter that the person may have expired long since. Extending forgiveness removes the legal grounds for the spirit of inherited lust to stay and that paves the way to command the spirit of inherited lust to leave. Even if the evidence is inconclusive that an inherited spirit of lust is present, I try to cover all bases and pray against an inherited spirit of lust anyway, because the person may not have all the facts. Sex sins are ordinarily not widely broadcast among all family members. If I happen to be wrong, nothing really has been lost.

After this process, I then go to the individual needs of the person I am praying for and command each afflicting sexual spirit to leave. When that is complete, I then command the spirit of lust to go, in Jesus' name. By this, I mean the spirit of lust that the person had invited in. This is a spirit different from the inherited spirit of lust. I treat them as two separate demons.

Incubus and Succubus

Inherited spirits of lust are frequently to blame for allowing the sexual spirits of Incubus and Succubus to operate while a person is asleep. What happens is that the person will have a very vivid dream in which he or she is approached by a "person" asking to have sex with him or her, or just doing it. The "person" may act in a heterosexual or homosexual manner and a sexual climax ensues as the individual awakens. The "person," if acting as a male, is not just a mental fantasy, but actually a demon called "Incubus," and if it acts as a female, it is a demon named "Succubus." I find these to be very foul, uninvited evil spirits that often, but not always, follow family lines. Some very bold ones will even attack a person during the day. When evicting them, call them by name and they often leave with a pronounced jolt in the body of their host. It seems as though their cover is shattered when they are called by name.

Compulsive Masturbation

Getting back to the problem of compulsive masturbation, I have prayed with men, in particular, for whom this is an all-consuming, ever-present issue. One man usually masturbated three times a day, and it was ruining his marriage because he was not paying attention to his wife. We then look for other clues and roots to the problem. Often the person has become addicted to pornography. Sometimes it is massive rejection of some sort. Frequently the person was sexually molested as a child or teen. It is very possible for a spirit of lust to take advantage of a sexual trauma, such as a rape, entering at that time - even though the victim was not seeking it. So we continue to gather information.

Clues were apparent in the above-mentioned man's case as to why the demon of compulsive masturbation was present. I don't remember them all, but I was clearly directed by God as to how to pray and he turned out to be an easy case. He was totally freed from the bondage and went home to announce the victory publicly to his friends. There are few more grateful people on Planet Earth than those who have been set free from long-standing bondages.

Ministering to the Whole Person

I find that praying for people with sexual bondages seem to fall into two broad categories. They are those who have invited problems into their lives, and those who have been victimized or seriously abused by caregivers or predators. The former are easy to pray for – those who have tears flowing down their cheeks and want to be free. They are so sorry for their sin and they want to repent and be healed of its consequences.

The latter, those who have been victimized, are extremely complex because a wide range of other very serious problems have often invaded. These might include things such as anger, hatred, self-hatred, suicidal tendencies, homosexuality, dissociative identity disorder (formerly called multiple personality disorder), misplaced affection, and a huge amount of other emotional damage that needs prolonged, tender care and healing as well as deliverance.

All too often deliverance ministers have not ministered to the "whole person," and the job should not be considered complete until the emotional aspect is healed as well. It is the better part of wisdom not to assume that just because evil spirits have been evicted that the task has been completed. If emotional healing is still needed, pray for what needs to be done, and refer the person to a pastor or counselor who can take them on from there.

Confidentiality

Two very important questions we continually keep in mind are (1) Why is this person afflicted? And (2) When did it begin? Usually probing these areas will reveal very important clues as to how to pray. It is vital that the person you are praying for disclose all information relevant to their problems. Partial disclosure is to be discouraged and a promise of confidentiality assured. This must never be violated. As a matter of fact, I do not keep information notes, usually in the form of a questionnaire, but I shred them in the presence of the person. To me, it helps them on their way to "Go and sin no more." What God has forgiven is forgiven, indeed.

Dealing with Guilt and Shame

As I have prayed for people with sexual bondages over the years, I find it very important to pray against two other related spirits. It is sometimes easy to forget, but I now make it a very important part of my prayers. These two evil spirits are "guilt" and "shame." Since my time is extremely limited due to being CEO of a Christian ministry, I am able to pray for just a few people, so I have chosen to pray for ministers. Most have no one to turn to when they seek deliverance for fear of losing their jobs or being embarrassed or exposed to their people. But I am safe. I don't know them and no one needs to know that a pastor has come to see me for deliverance.

One thing that truly bothers pastors with sexual problems that are demonic in nature is that they are called to preach the Word of God. But how can they preach against sex sins if they are victims themselves? They feel like such hypocrites! So I must always remember to pray against the spirits of guilt and shame so that the pastor can then preach as he or she must. Those condemning spirits have to leave. The Bible has a great deal of instruction concerning keeping oneself pure and a congregation desperately needs this teaching.

Deliverance; Then Restoration

I recently prayed deliverance over a minister who had been divorced and since that experience, he has not been allowed to have
a pastorate in his denomination. I find myself disagreeing with
this policy for several reasons. First of all, I think of Mary
Magdalene in Scripture who, after having been cleansed from seven
demons became one of those very grateful persons to follow and
serve Jesus. There is some disagreement as to whether some of
those evil spirits may have been sexual in nature, but no matter.
Because of the social position of women in that century, I am deeply
touched by the fact that Jesus appeared to this formerly demonized
woman first after His resurrection, as though she were someone
very important and that He cared for her. Mark 16:9 says "Now
when He rose early on the first day of the week, He appeared first
to Mary Magdalene, out of whom He had cast seven demons."

The point I am trying to make is that once Mary Magdalene
had been cleansed from demons, it would appear that Jesus did not
hold past failure against her, but accepted her appreciation and
devotion, and gave her the chance to start over. If a person, such as
the pastor I refer to above, has been cleansed from his past and
shows fruit of repentance, why should he be forever removed from
ministry? It does not seem to follow the example of Jesus' treatment of Mary Magdalene. Jesus didn't rebuke Mary for following
Him and even serving Him as though she were some sort of second
class citizen.

I told that pastor to try to start a church among divorced persons, since so very many marriages end in shipwreck. Many of
those wounded people would never darken the door of a church
because they feel like social outcasts and someone needs to present
them with the gospel. And who better understands broken mar-

riages than a person who has gone through the pain and has come out of the other side healed?

Pray Cleansing

The last thing I do when praying over a person who has been infested with evil sexual spirits is to pray cleansing over him or her. I ask God to miraculously cleanse that person's mind of pornographic images and ungodly sexual experiences. I also ask God to cleanse the eyes that have looked upon what they should not have, to cleanse the ears from what has been heard, to cleanse the mouth, the skin, the hands, and the sexual organs from all sinful thoughts, words, and deeds. It is extremely important to break all soul ties with sex partners who are not the person's spouse. (Peter Horrobin deals eloquently with this topic in Chapter Three.) I ask God for their current marriage relationship, that it be as God intended, complete with joy and sexual fulfillment.

Those of us in the deliverance ministry delight in seeing people made whole again. It is a great embarrassment to Satan who has come to steal, kill, and destroy. And we really enjoy being part of setting those captives free. We see great potential in any person who wants deliverance and our prayer is that many will benefit from being set free from sexual bondages and go on to serve the Lord with all of their being.

"Jesus answered 'whoever commits sin is a slave of sin. Therefore, if the Son makes you free, you shall be free indeed'" (John 8:34, 36).

Chapter Two

Sexual Sin: What It Is, What It Does, and Finding the Way Out

Peter Horrobin

Peter Horrobin is the International Director of Ellel Ministries. After graduating at Oxford, he spent many years in University lecturing, writing and publishing before the work was founded in 1986. Since then it has steadily expanded, both in the UK and other countries. There are now three teaching and ministry centers in England, one in Canada, and a major pioneering work in Eastern Europe. The team now numbers over 140 people. Among many other publications, he has written an excellent two volume book entitled *Healing Through Deliverance*. Peter and his wife, Fiona, live near Ellel Grange in Lancashire, England. For more information on the ministry or available resources, please write Ellel Ministries, Ellel Grange, Ellel, Lancaster, LA2 0HN, England or visit www.ellel.org.

It is impossible to understand the nature and consequences of sexual sin without first understanding what God's original plan and purpose was for the human race. Then, from within an understanding of God's creative purposes we can begin to understand His plan and purpose for marriage and then sex within marriage.

Made to be Creative

We are made in the image and likeness of God. God is spirit and, therefore, we are also spiritual beings. But God is also creative, being the Creator, and the spirit with us is, therefore, creative by nature.

But we are more than a spirit; we are also creatures of flesh. And flesh is more than just the body, for without there being a part of us which gives the body instructions, the body would be incapable of functioning effectively. The soul is that part of us which gives the body its instructions.

A body without a soul would be a bit like a car without a driver. Just as a car only moves when instructed to do so by its driver, the body only moves when acted upon by the soul. And just as a bad driver is capable of damaging the vehicle and causing it to be a danger to themselves, other cars and other people, so the soul is capable of leading the body into dangerous territory, both endangering itself, and being a danger to others.

Our complete entity is, therefore, spirit, soul, and body. It is through the spirit that we are able to fellowship with God. The soul stands at the interface between the spirit and the body. The soul and the body together are what the Bible refers to as the flesh and which enables us to function as human beings. The spirit and the soul together form what we broadly call the personality of a human being.

Creativity lies at the center of the human spirit, and God intended that it should find its expression in human beings through the flesh (the body and the soul). Whenever we use the gifts that God has given for Godly purposes it is, indirectly, an act of worship of the God who made us.

So when a child makes a tower out of wooden blocks, or an architect designs a building, they are expressing their God-given creativity. When an artist paints a picture, an author writes a book, or a chef prepares a meal, they are also expressing something of the creative gifting they received into their spirit from their Creator. Godly sex within the covenant of marriage rejoices the heart of God. So when a husband and wife express themselves in godly sexual relationship, it is both an expression of human creativity and an act of worship to God!

The Challenge of Freewill

When God made us, however, He risked everything by also giving us the gift of freewill. God was desirous of a relationship with us that is an expression of love, which means, among other things, that God desires a relationship that is entered into through the exercise of freewill choice, not one that is enforced through domination and control. But this also means that all the creative gifts God has given us can be used for good or evil purposes.

An architect, for example, who is capable of designing a magnificent and inspiring cathedral could also use that creative gifting to design such awful things as the gas chambers of Auschwitz. An artist can use brushes to paint a picture of exquisite beauty, but can also use the same brushes to paint a scene of unimaginable filth, horror, and degradation. A film director can inspire, challenge, and entertain with a movie of extraordinary power and sensitivity or use the same skills to drag viewers into mental participation in violence, pornography, and distaste.

Sadly, there is no limit to the behavior extremes of the fallen human race. Throughout history humanity has plumbed the depths of behavior that is an abomination to a holy God. None more so is this the case than in the realm of sexuality, where ungodly desires of the soul can so easily take precedence over the desires of the spirit. The unredeemed have no spiritual brakes to apply to their behavior. They become wise in their own eyes and *"I'll do it my way"* becomes the theme song of a world without God.

Only now, with the onset of a worldwide AIDS crisis of epidemic proportions, is the world having the opportunity to reassess some of the physical consequences of removing restraints on sexual behavior. Tragically, the world's preferred response is not to discourage ungodly sexual activity through a return to godly order, but to encourage further indulgence in Satan's counterfeit regime through an even wider availability of cheap or free protective contraceptives, not solely for contraceptive purposes, but so as to limit the extent of disease transmission during heterosexual intercourse or homosexual relationships.

The world is only concerned about the physical dangers of un-protected sex. The god of this world has so blinded their eyes that the spiritual dangers of ungodly sex have become irrelevant to a godless and politically correct society (where there are no abso-lutes and every faith or belief system, and moral code or lack of it, has to be given equal political standing, and where Christian truth is made to take its place as a supposed "equal" alongside every other false religion, including witchcraft and atheism).

The Spiritual Dangers of Ungodly Sex

The spiritual dangers of ungodly sex are such that no contraceptive in the world can ever provide protection against them. And many of those inside the church are seemingly ignorant of the spiritual consequences of sexual sin. I say seemingly ignorant, because if they were fully aware of the dangers, teaching in the church would at least match the teaching that is abundantly evident throughout Scripture, and the incidence of sexual sin in the church would be significantly less than it actually is.

In reality there is so much sexual sin inside the body of Christ that, on occasions, it is hard to distinguish between the sexual prac-tices of believers and unbelievers! Instead of the church being "salt and light" in the world, the world has been allowed to sow poison inside the church. And so lightly is sexual sin often per-ceived that, for many, the Bible's teaching on sex and sexuality is dismissed as out-of-date, or even irrelevant, for the permissive age in which we live. I have even had it said to me that they believed the Bible's teaching was true for earlier ages, but now that we have developed reliable contraceptives, biblical requirements for sexual conduct are no longer appropriate.

And even in those sectors of the church where there is clear and unequivocal teaching on what is right and wrong sexual conduct, there is little understanding of the spiritual consequences of sexual sin, leaving people ignorant of the reasons why purity truly

> ## The spiritual dangers of ungodly sex are such that no contraceptive in the world can ever provide protection against them. And many of those inside the church are seemingly ignorant of the spiritual consequences of sexual sin.

is God's best for His creation. When teaching on the subject, I have found that when people understand what happens when we sin sexually, they come under the conviction of the Holy Spirit, see the need for cleansing and quickly come to the place of open confession and repentance.

It is not for nothing that Paul went out of his way to emphasize this point by telling the Christians in Corinth to, "Flee from sexual immorality. All other sins a man commits are outside his body, but he who sins sexually sins against his own body" (1 Cor. 6:18, NIV). As we will see later, sexual sin gives the enemy rights within the body through ungodly soul ties.

We live in a rebellious age when respect for authority is no longer enough to restrain the behavior of the willful and, sadly,

within the church respect for the authority of Scripture has dimin-
ished. It is no longer enough to restrain the sexual behavior of
believers, let alone unbelievers. The church may have become
more exciting and more charismatic, but in so doing it seems to
have lost something of the fear of the Lord. And as is so clearly
expressed in Exodus 20:20, "the fear of God will be with you to
keep you from sinning" (NIV). Nothing else will keep people from
sinning when a person is alone and there is no expectation that
anyone else will see what they are doing.

The Bible's teaching on sowing and reaping has been largely
sidelined. Paul warned about not letting the grace of God become
an excuse for sinful indulgence. The born-again believer (one whose
spirit has been restored again to fellowship with God through faith
in Jesus Christ) living in a fallen world will never in this life be
free from temptation. The age-old battle between the will of the
spirit and the will of the soul (the flesh) is described graphically by
Paul in Galatians 5.

Paul warned in verse 21 that "those who practice such things
shall not inherit the kingdom of God" (NIV). Understanding the
difference between godly and ungodly sex and then choosing to
walk in God's ways, could indeed be a matter of life and death.
The writer of the Proverbs (2:18) warns that the house of the adul-
teress "leads down to death and her paths to the spirits of the dead"
(NIV).

So what actually is adultery? Jeremiah 3 provides us with a
powerful insight into God's understanding of adultery. Here the
peoples of Judah and Israel are accused of committing adultery
with stone and wood (vv. 8 to 10). Not because they were having
ungodly sex, but because they were worshipping idols, worshipping a false god. They were joining themselves through worship

to another god. Jehovah was their true God but they were going after another.

Adultery is, therefore, all wrongful joining together. By this definition, all sexual sin, be it before marriage, after marriage, in homosexual relationships or even with animals is defined as being adulterous. Which means that the seventh commandment, "You shall not commit adultery" (Ex. 20:14, NIV), has a much wider meaning than just heterosexual sin by married people. It embraces all forms of ungodly sexual relationships.

As this chapter unfolds the full spiritual dangers of sexual sin will become clear. My prayer is that as people begin to understand, they will find themselves on a road to restoration and healing.

Healing Grace and Mercy

Although the Scriptures face the reality of the fact that even believers can fall into sexual sin and are clear on what is right and wrong, they are also full of hope, telling us of a God who longs to forgive and to heal. God's promise is that when His people humble themselves, truly confess their sin, repent and turn from their sin, that He will forgive and restore. While what has been done cannot be undone, David's account of his encounter with God, following the exposure of his adultery with Bathsheba, is eloquent testimony to God's mercy and healing grace (see Ps. 51).

It is absolutely clear, from both Scripture and experience, that when we choose to walk in the ways of the god of this world, we open the door to the enemy, which means that those who have knowingly walked in sexual sin not only need to repent, ask for forgiveness, and change their ways, but will also need deliverance in order to enter into the full healing that God wants them to have.

We cannot sweep these facts under the spiritual carpet. But we do need to be careful to respect the attitude of Jesus towards the woman who was caught in an act of adultery. Her accusers were ready to stone her to death, but Jesus had compassion upon her. It is easy to be judgmental without understanding.

The first time I ministered to a prostitute, I was aware of an inner anger at what this twenty-three-year-old woman had done to men. When I asked how long she had been a prostitute, and she told me thirteen years, I began to reassess my thinking. When she told me how her father had left home, her mother had little money, and how she was led into child prostitution by a man who offered her sweets, and then money, for letting him touch her, I began to weep at the terrible damage that had been done by unscrupulous evil men. I finished up repenting to her on behalf of men for what they had done to her.

We must be very careful not to fall into Satan's trap of heaping condemnation on those who have sinned sexually. There is hope, there is forgiveness, there is deliverance, and there is healing.

Made for Relationship

As explained by Doris Wagner in Chapter 1, God designed man and woman for each other and provided them with the means through which they should not only express their relationship spiritually and emotionally, but also physically. God's intention for sexual expression between husband and wife was that this should be the highpoint of human relationship – a deeply spiritual experience of extraordinary oneness – indeed, so spiritual that the same Hebrew word is used to describe sexual relationships between human beings as to describe the intimacy and depth of spiritual relationship that we as humans are able to have with the living God.

Sex was designed by God to be so enjoyable that the development of the human race through sexual reproduction would never be in doubt! Through the expression of their sexuality, God allows men and women to share with Him in an act of creation. And sex as God originally intended, between unfallen man and unfallen woman, was, therefore, a glorious act of worship of the creator God.

While man's body has the physical capacity for casual, animal-like sex with any female, without the requirement of commitment to a relationship, the idea of casual sex is totally foreign to God's plan for humankind. There is nowhere in Scripture where any expression of casual sex, or sex outside of the marriage covenant, is approved of or encouraged. This is, however, the spirit of the age in which we are now living, where hedonism, unrestricted self-seeking pleasure, is rampant throughout much of the world's society.

Understanding that godly sexual expression is a form of worship is a vital key to understanding why sexual sin leads people into sexual and demonic bondage. For God rejoices to bless His people with His spiritual presence, especially when they are worshipping Him. The early forms of the marriage service included a reference to adoration and worship, when in the vows with which the couple would commit themselves to each other they say these words, "with my body I, thee, worship."

Whenever we make freewill choices to please Him, we put ourselves in the place of God's blessing being upon us. And there is no doubt that God rejoices to pour His blessing on godly sexual relationships within the covenant of marriage.

The converse of this, however, is that in this fallen world Satan takes advantage of the fact that we were made to worship, and that in worship we make ourselves open to the spiritual. Satan welcomes it when we indulge in sexual practices which are contrary to God's order, because then it is not the living God that is being worshipped, but Satan. God will not give His glory to another and He will not, therefore, remain on the throne of a relationship that is ungodly. He cannot bless or rejoice in those things that are contrary to His created order for humanity.

So, as the god of this world, Satan steps onto the throne of the relationship and receives the worship. But far from blessing the participants, who are pleasing Satan with their ungodly use of their creative sexuality, he uses the opportunity to bring them his cursing. And the spirits with which Satan indwells people are not holy, but unholy, or as the gospel writers describe them, unclean. Through sexual sin, they are able to access the body which Scripture tells us is, or should be, the "temple of the Holy Spirit" (1 Cor. 6:19, NIV).

Guilt and Shame

Before the fall there was no sin and, therefore, no guilt or shame. Guilt and shame are what we feel when we have caused offense to someone else through our behavior, especially when that someone else is God. In the absence of any other being, there cannot be any feeling of guilt or shame. The very fact that people are aware of guilt and shame is primary evidence of the existence of God.

Guilty is what we are as a consequence of an offense we have committed. Guilt is resolved through restitution and forgiveness. Jesus paid the price for our sin and through forgiveness we are absolved of the consequences of our sin.

Shame is what we feel on the inside when we have sinned. Shame makes us want to hide from those we have let down, hurt, betrayed, or sinned against. A young boy will instinctively want to hide from his parents when he knows he has done something wrong, just as Adam and Eve tried to cover themselves up and hide from God in the garden.

Shame can only be healed when the sin that caused the shame has been brought to the light and forgiven. There are some people whose whole lives are lived behind a wall of shame. Sometimes the shame is as a result of what they have done, but often it is a consequence of what others have done to them. A girl who has been sexually abused can feel the shame of what was experienced, especially when an abuser lays the blame for what has happened on the victim, without being guilty in any way for what happened. Satan will always try and use shame to prevent people from stretching out their hands and asking for help.

Jesus is the only One who can touch and heal the person living with the consequences of shame in the heart. He paid the price for our sin, made it possible for us to be freed from the curse of other people's sin against us (through forgiving them) and know the reality of His healing presence, changing us from the inside out.

Chapter Three

Shedding Light on Soul Ties

Peter Horrobin

God's intentions for sexual fulfillment lie strictly within the covenant of marriage. Marriage is not just a legal transaction. It is primarily a spiritual transaction – a joining together of two people. Just as man (and woman) are spirit, soul, and body, then God also intended the covenant of marriage to lead to a permanent union of spirit, soul, and body.

A couple who intend to marry may be spiritually joined in faith, heart, and intent, but until after the vows have been made to each other and to God, and intercourse has taken place, the marriage is not complete. Indeed, the church has always recognized that a marriage which has not been completed with sexual intercourse is one that can be annulled – for it is not a proper marriage. Intercourse is the union of flesh, when the desire of the soul is completed through bodily sexual union. Through sexual union, therefore, there is both a joining of spirit and soul and a joining of bodies.

After intercourse has taken place, the bodies separate, but the souls are now joined together – the marriage, as such, is complete. There is then not only a union of spirit, but also a union of soul. Scripture talks about the two having become one flesh (Eph. 5:31). There is now a soul tie established between husband and wife through the act of sexual union. Something of the man becomes part of the woman and something of the woman becomes part of the man. It is for this reason that as the years go by, married couples can grow like each other in so many different ways. Even to the extent that it is sometimes possible to see the effect physically in couples that have been married for a long time.

What we have now established is that the physical union of sexual intercourse involves more than the physical joining of bodies, for those who have been joined together in this way also become joined together in their souls with what we call a *soul tie*. This was God's wonderful plan for marriage, permanently uniting couples in a living and dynamic relationship.

Consequences of Sexual Sin

We established in the last chapter that when people enter into sexual sin, they are pleasing the god of this world and, as a result, they may have welcomed an unclean spirit into their lives for which deliverance is needed. We have now understood that God's intention for marriage was to provide a means through which man and woman would be permanently united in spirit and soul. Paul even tells us that God's intentions for the relationship between husband and wife could even be used as a picture of God's intentions for the relationship between Jesus and the church! (see Eph. 5). That's the good news!

The bad news for those who are sexually promiscuous is that God does not suspend His plans to establish a soul tie between them in order to accommodate their sin. While God is undoubtedly a God of love, He is also a God of law and order, and God's order for sexual relationships is that *whenever* they occur, a joining takes place and a soul tie is established.

So if a person, for example, had several sexual partners in their youth, he (or she) now has a soul tie with each one of these. Something of themselves has been given away to each sexual partner and something of the other person has become part of them. Paul explicitly stated that this is even so in the case of prostitution, where he says that when a man unites himself with a prostitute "the two will become one flesh" (1 Cor. 6:16, NIV).

Instead of this being a godly soul tie, which brings great blessing into the lives of a husband and wife, it becomes a chain of bondage through which people are influenced unknowingly by the life and personality of those to whom they have been sexually joined. Furthermore, an ungodly soul tie provides an opportunity for the demonic to transfer from one person to another, both at the time of sexual intercourse and at any time subsequent.

The whole of Proverbs 5 is a warning against adulterous sexual relationships. Verse 22 sums up the consequences of ungodly sex by saying that "the evil deeds of a wicked man ensnare him; the cords of his sin hold him fast" (NIV). An ungodly soul tie is a cord of sin which holds people in permanent bondage – at least until Jesus breaks the chain. Because it is through God's order for humankind that a soul tie was established in the first place, it follows that it is only God who can undo it.

Breaking the Chains of Ungodly Soul Ties

First John 1:9 encourages us to confess our sins to God so that we will be forgiven. But in James 5:16, Scripture tells us to "confess your sins to each other and pray for each other so that you may be healed" (NIV). There are clearly two processes going on. One deals with the eternal, spiritual consequence of sin and the restoration of relationship with God through forgiveness, and the other deals with the temporal consequences of sin which have caused a condition requiring healing – healing that can include the need for deliverance.

Of course God can (and does) heal some people sovereignly when they pray to Him. But for many people there may also be a pride issue that has to be dealt with, and it is only the process of telling someone else about the sin that deals with the pride, which is sometimes a major blockage to receiving healing. We have seen this to be especially the case in respect to sexual sin in Christians. People would prefer not to experience the shame of someone else knowing about their sin. But where there is a pride issue in the heart, it is the humbling of oneself in this way that enables God to lift us up, restore us fully into His presence, and release us into healing and fulfillment of the calling He has for us.

There is no sin that God is not able to forgive – and ultimately it is only He that can wipe our slate clean. Similarly, it is only God that can undo those soul ties that have been established through ungodly sexual relationships. So in a ministry situation we would encourage a person to confess their sin to God, asking Him for forgiveness and restoration, and then we would ask God to break the ungodly soul tie and restore the person to a place where that which they gave away to another in a wrong relationship is restored to them, and they are completely released of everything that came to them from their sexual partners.

The effect of this can be very profound, bringing transformation to people's lives as they are restored to being the person that God intended them to be in the first place. The final part of the ministry is the deliverance. While we have to ask God to bring the healing (severing) of ungodly soul ties, Jesus gave to believers authority to cast out demons. It is our general experience that where there have been ungodly sexual soul ties, there will also have been demons that either came in at the time of the sin or which have used the soul tie to enter subsequently.

Stories from the Casebook

Some of the real-life stories, gained from our experience within Ellel Ministries, will help you understand the significance of soul ties and the importance of not allowing any of the works of darkness to remain uncleansed in a person's life.

One man I ministered to freely confessed that he had had about fifty sexual partners. The Holy Spirit had brought deep conviction of the sin in his life and he was truly repentant. After he had fully confessed the sins and asked God to forgive him, I then asked God to break the ungodly soul ties and restore him on the inside. Prior to this incident, the man had had no teaching on the subject to influence how he would describe what happened. This is what he said: "It feels as though there are parts of me coming back to me. And I can see things that I thought were part of who I am, disappearing as God takes them away." Then he made a very profound statement, "For the first time that I can remember, I know who I am!" He was rediscovering his own true identity. One of the major consequences of sexual sin is that, through the establishment of ungodly soul ties, we begin to lose our own identity. And the more partners with whom an individual has had sex, the less they know who they really are.

In reality, until God had dealt with the ungodly soul ties this man couldn't have known who he was, for he was joined to fifty other people, all of whom were having some sort of an influence on his life. And at the same time, it was as if his own influence was being spread around the world in the lives of all those with whom he had had sex. After God had broken the ungodly ties, he was free to be himself for the first time since he had begun to be promiscuous as a teenager. The final part of the ministry was deliverance and, not surprisingly, there was a lot of deliverance needed.

Another man, who was a pastor of a local church, came to me concerned that he was unable to make any more headway in his church. It seemed as though every time he tried to move things forward along the pathway of renewal, an impenetrable blockage stood in the way. When I first asked him about previous sexual partners he was surprised by the question, not thinking that this could have any relevance to his situation. He freely admitted that before he was a Christian he had been quite promiscuous and, yes, there had been ten different sexual partners. But he had totally turned his back on this lifestyle following his conversion and he believed that had all been dealt with at the cross.

I explained to him that the sin was totally forgiven and that God had wiped the record of the sin off the slate. But in reality there is also a law of sowing and reaping and not only does sin have to be confessed and repented of to deal with the eternal consequences, but there are times when cleansing and healing are also necessary to deal with the consequences in time.

He understood what I was saying and gladly wrote down the names of the ten girls. One by one I prayed through the list asking

God to break the ungodly soul ties. And one by one he sensed God doing a profound work of cleansing on the inside and after each one significant deliverance took place. Until, that is we reached number five. I only just began to pronounce her name with the syllable "Ang," when I was stunned by a violent and noisy demonic response from the man as he shouted out at me, *"You are not having her!"* He was just as stunned as I was and, after he had recovered his composure, I asked him what he could remember about Angela.

He had no difficulty in remembering that Angela was always dressed in black and was actively involved in witchcraft. Here was the major key to the blockage he was experiencing in his ministry. He was bonded to someone whose witchcraft was still being used against him through the ungodly soul tie which had been established all those years earlier. Satan uses every possible hook to try and limit the effectiveness of our ministries. Having prayed to bind the demons of witchcraft, they were silenced. God broke that soul tie forever and he was a different man after that. The remaining soul ties and subsequent deliverance presented no problem.

A lady once told me that there was a night in her marriage when she sensed there was someone else present in the bed with her and her husband. She couldn't understand why she was feeling so repulsed by his presence. He had been away on business and she had been looking forward to restoration of intimate relationships with him on his return.

But there was something wrong and she knew it. It was only years later she found out that when her husband had been away he had committed adultery. What his wife had been sensing was the presence of the other woman, to whom her husband was now joined with an ungodly soul tie. For years since that moment, their relationship had been tarnished by the spiritual presence of the other woman.

Over the years we have ministered freedom from ungodly sexual soul ties to countless thousands of people around the world; from every racial grouping and from most nations. The fruit has been remarkable. Often Satan uses the ungodly soul ties to hold individuals into demonic symptoms of physical illness, preventing them from ever being fully whole. Demonic transference in this way is one of the most common sources of sickness in the body of Christ.

We have frequently prayed for people who have had previous sexual partners and, after prayer and deliverance, they have experienced a significant measure of healing. Sometimes the effect has

God's order for sexual relationships is that *whenever* they occur, a joining takes place and a soul tie is established.

been quite dramatic as symptoms a person may have been wrestling with for years are suddenly healed as ungodly ties are broken.

On one occasion I taught a large church about the nature of sexual sin and its consequences. When teaching in this way I often use drama to graphically illustrate the key points. I have a young couple on the platform who, in the drama, are about to get married, and I then expose the fact that they have both had previous sexual partners. In the drama these previous partners are hanging onto the young couple as they prepare to get married. But these previous partners have also had other sexual relationships, so there is a second generation of ties, and a third and so on. When people see just how many different people are tied into the marriage, they realize how dangerous sexual sin is and they understand why the Scriptures are so clear about the need for sexual purity both before and after marriage.

After the church had seen the drama and heard the teaching, I then opened up the front of the church for confession, repentance, and ministry. A flood of people came forward. There were many tears, as well as major deliverance and a great amount of physical healing as the holds of the enemy on these dear people's lives was broken forever. The pastors of the church looked on in amazement. They thought they knew their people and were deeply shocked at the extent of need in this area among their people.

One lady came for prayer because she was unable to conceive a child with her husband. On asking a few questions, I found out that there had been a previous boyfriend who wanted to marry her, but whom she had given up to marry the man she really loved. Her previous boyfriend, however, with whom she had been having sexual relations, was both heartbroken and very angry. He vowed that she would never have a child by another man.

Such words were, in fact, a curse which Satan could use to release demons against her – in this case a spirit of death – to prevent her ever being able to have her own child. The soul tie between them gave the enemy easy access to her life. It was only when the soul tie had been broken, and she had been delivered of the spirit of death, that she was then able to conceive.

It has become a common experience for us to minister in this way to women who, for various reasons, are currently unable to conceive. We often find that in earlier life they had had other sexual partners and, in some cases, had had an abortion after becoming pregnant. What a joy it is to bring healing to such people through first dealing with the sin of abortion, and then asking God to break all the ungodly soul ties, followed by deliverance from all the unclean spirits. The icing on the cake is to subsequently receive a photograph of the longed-for baby! We have many such pictures in our files. They are a constant encouragement as we press on to bring healing to God's people.

Special Situations

All that I have said so far about the need for confession, repentance, breaking of soul ties, and deliverance applies to all forms of sexual sin which have been entered into through the freewill choice of the participants.

The primary difference between those who have committed sexual sin before marriage (fornication) and those who have committed sexual sin after marriage (adultery) is that the latter also involves betrayal of the marriage covenant with one's wife or husband, with all the possible consequences of secondary pain and relationship breakdown. Ministry into the marital relationship or into the consequences of relationship breakdown is beyond the scope of this chapter.

It is increasingly common to find that married couples who have a godly sexual relationship within marriage, began their sexual relationship with fornication before marriage. In these cases there can be both an ungodly and a godly soul tie between the couple.

It is necessary for the ungodly dimension of the relationship to be fully dealt with, for this can be a source of spiritual friction or even be the grounds for an unclean spirit to cause sexual problems and division in the relationship through temptation to subsequent sexual sin. One lady in this situation was radically healed of epilepsy, which had started at the time of her marriage. Having dealt with the fornication she was then delivered and wonderfully healed.

Abuse and Rape

Where sexual relationships were forced upon a person in an abusive or rape situation, an ungodly soul tie is still established between the abuser or the rapist and their victim, even though the relationship was against the will of the victim. While there is always much deeper ministry that is required in order to take the person through the issue of forgiveness and healing for the terrible betrayal and ordeal they have experienced, it is still necessary at some point in the ministry to deal with the ungodly soul ties.

Many people who have been abused in their early days, have come to believe that they would never be free of intrusive memories of their ordeal and the perpetrator. It was only after God had broken the soul ties that they were free to move on in their healing without being chained to the person who had stolen so much from them through what was done.

Those who have been abused or raped will also need help with the shame associated with their ordeal. While, in reality, there may be nothing they have done which merits personal guilt or shame, one of Satan's tactics is to overwhelm the person with what is false guilt and false shame, often demonically empowered, which entraps the person into a false identity from which it is very difficult for them to escape without the help of those who can take them by the hand and see them restored under the hand of God. In severe cases, there can also be a breaking of the personality requiring much more in-depth personal ministry.

Perversion

Perverted sex is everything that God would define as being ungodly sexual conduct, beyond the practice of heterosexual relationships. This would include sex with animals, homosexual and lesbian relationships, oral sex where a woman is made to experience her partner's ejaculation into her mouth, sexual violence and punishment, and all forms of ritual sex.

The teaching that anything goes within marriage, provided that both partners agree to it, finds no place in Scripture. Perverted sexual practices are wrong, whether they are found inside or outside of marriage. I never cease to be amazed at the extremes of sexual behavior that some people have experimented with. It is little surprise that they are struggling with all manner of spiritual, emotional, physical, and sexual problems and temptations. There is no way out except through uncompromising honesty, a radical determination to turn from all such behavior, deliverance, and healing.

Sometimes people have been led into perverted sexual conduct by someone else. For example, a person may have been encouraged to experiment with animal sex by a particular individual. It is our experience that in cases such as this there is often a soul tie between the participants, even though they may not have had direct personal sexual contact. The agreement together to participate in ungodliness is enough to join them together in an ungodly soul tie.

Pornography

Pornography of all types provides the means for individuals to participate lustfully, through the eyes, in other people's sexually promiscuous or perverted behavior. Jesus faced this possibility head on in Matthew 5:28 when He said that, "anyone who looks on a woman lustfully has already committed adultery with her in his heart" (NIV).

The use of pornography as an aid to masturbation highlights the sexual joining in the mind there can be with the image that is being looked at, resulting in a physical sexual expression. It may be necessary when ministering to those for whom pornography has become an uncontrollable force in their life to ask God to break the soul ties that have been established through the mind with the images people have lustfully used.

None of us can escape the gratuitous onslaught of sexual images that bombard us through all branches of the media, especially through television and films. Satan uses this constant bombardment to try and wear us down so that they become increasingly tolerant of watching blatantly ungodly images. We need to be constantly on our guard to this and learn to resist the devil's temptations whenever they face us.

And, Finally...

There are many people who have desperately tried secretly, and in their own strength, to overcome the temptations of the enemy in the sexual area. Often, largely because they have been ignorant of the nature of the battle, they have not had access to the weapons with which to fight. But once people understand the true nature of sexual sin, soul ties, and the need for deliverance, it is as though a huge obstacle to their healing has been removed.

However, deliverance should not be considered as the end of the story. We still have to exercise our freewill in order to remain free through making godly choices for, as Peter tells us very graphically, "Your enemy the devil prowls round like a roaring lion looking for someone to devour" (1 Pet. 5:8, NIV), which means that Satan doesn't generally give up on trying to tempt us! Peter's simple advice is to "Resist him, standing firm in the faith" (1 Pet. 5:9,

NIV). For as long as we resist him, the enemy cannot have any ground to stand on in our lives.

May the Lord give you His understanding of any issues you are personally facing and enable you to receive any necessary healing and deliverance so that you will then have the strength to stand firm as you choose to walk in obedience and fellowship with Him.

Chapter Four

The Effects of Lust on Youth

Tim and Anne Evans

Tim and Anne are Deans of School for Real Life Academy, a division of Wagner Leadership Institute. Beginning fall of 2004 in Colorado Springs, Colorado, this school will focus on spiritual parenting, equipping, and mentoring the eighteen to twenty-nine age group. Happily married for twenty-seven years, they have four grown children. Tim and Anne both served as lay leaders for almost twenty years at Willow Creek Community Church. Tim served on the fire department in Schaumburg, Illinois and retired as Deputy Fire Chief. They were then called to Lakeland Community Church in Holland, Michigan where they were ordained and served for five years. They relocated to Pasadena, California and served as Deans of Students for the inaugural Wagner Leadership Institute – The Call School. They both graduated from Wagner Leadership Institute with diplomas in Master of Practical Ministry.

*For all that is in the world—the **lust** of the flesh and the **lust** of the eyes and the boastful pride of life, is not from the Father, but is from the world* (1 John 2:16, NAS, emphasis added).

It was supposed to be the standard question and answer session. After years of speaking to married couples on the topic of intimacy and sexuality, we were excited about the opportunity to present this subject to a younger group. Their ages ranged anywhere from fourteen to eighteen years old. After working through our outline, we planned to end the night with this session. As our experience grew, it seemed we were almost able to predict the kind of questions that would be asked. Offering biblical principles and godly counsel, we hoped that listeners would be better equipped to make informed choices, reflecting the character of God.

There was a box near the podium filled with questions that the students had written out. Reaching in to pull out the first card, we began, "This is from a 15-year-old female and she asks (long pause),

"If you want to stay a virgin, is anal sex okay?" An awkward silence filled the room before it was broken by the embarrassed giggle of a few girls in the front row. The older students seemed unaffected, as they quietly waited for our response.

Masking the surprise that was generated, we proceeded to respond. It wasn't the question that shocked us; it was the question *behind* the question. What that 15-year-old girl was really asking us was, "Is it okay, with God, if I engage in *another kind* of sexual activity, one that would allow me to keep my virginity, and technically not break God's law?"

Satan loves to take full advantage of a child's immaturity and lack of biblical understanding. By reclassifying anal sex as *another kind* of sexual activity, a child could easily be convinced that this perversion is an acceptable option. Anytime students begin to

Sexual promiscuity, rooted in a spirit of lust, continues to inflict the kind of soul-wounding that cries out for deliverance and inner healing.

focus on the letter of the law by looking for loopholes that could vindicate sinful behavior, it is not long before they are justifying actions that fall outside of God's original design. The question that we often hear from students regarding sexual behavior is, *how far can I go sexually and still fall within God's perimeter?* The question we want to encourage them to ask is, *what is God's best for me?*

When we were growing up, the issue of anal sex would have been classified as a twisted act, considered only by sexual deviants. The idea of sodomy being a substitute for intercourse for the purpose of maintaining one's virginity would have never even occurred to us. And even if it had, it would not have been a topic for public discussion at a Christian youth group gathering. We have become so desensitized by sin that distortions are becoming more and more acceptable.

Communicating with our youth is the key to keeping a healthy, strong and growing relationship. It is so important that children hear an accurate and honest view of God's original design for their life and for their sexuality. If we can pray and live out opportunities to introduce them to their Father, they will be able to recognize the father of lies. If we can pray and live out opportunities for His design to be taught, it will be easier for them to spot the counterfeit.

Let us behave properly as in the day, not in carousing and drunkenness, not in sexual promiscuity and sensuality, not in strife and jealousy. But put on the Lord Jesus Christ, and make no provision for the flesh in regard to its lusts (Rom. 13:13-14, NAS).

Recent statistics reinforce what we are seeing in this generation: sixty-one percent of all high school seniors have had sexual intercourse; about half are currently sexually active; and twenty-one percent have had four or more partners. The United States has one of the highest teenage pregnancy rates in the world. About a quarter of all sexually active adolescents become infected with a sexually transmitted disease (STD) each year. [1]

While these statistics are compelling, we do not need research companies to tell us values and moral codes are becoming increasingly ambiguous. Students are bombarded with distortions of sex in almost every facet of their lives. Everywhere they turn, the enemy is introducing images that open a door to lust-at school, in the workplace, on television, on the Internet, over the radio, and at the movies. The enemy's plan to deceive an entire generation is working. Is it any wonder that he targets our youth? Young children in their formative years are easily deceived, inexperienced, and naïve. For the most part, they are unaware of the spiritual battle that is raging for their hearts and souls.

Our evening with the youth group continued as each new question evoked a lively discussion: *Can I get an STD if my boyfriend wears a rubber? What are sex toys? Is masturbation a sin? Why doesn't the church ever talk about this stuff? Is it a sin to lust if you don't do anything about it? Why does sex always feel dirty even when the Bible says God created it? Is it wrong to look at the Internet sites that pop up on your screen, if you didn't type them in?*

Spiritual Fathers and Mothers

During a break time, a young girl asked to talk to us. She expressed her appreciation for the honest and straightforward discussion. She ended by saying, "No wonder we are so confused. Nobody ever talks to us about this stuff." It was a privilege for us to plow through this new ground together. Our interaction with the students made us more aware than ever of the need for godly spiritual fathers and mothers being God's voice speaking into the lives of this younger generation, helping them build a strong foundation for living well. Is it difficult? Yes! Discipleship means imparting your very life, but the rewards have eternal impact. It is not wisdom that qualifies us as spiritual parents, it is love.

It was the apostle Paul who said, "We have 10,000 teachers but not many spiritual fathers" (1 Cor. 4:15, NAS). His words have never been more true, nor the need greater, than for this generation. Working with youth reinforces our need to continue crying out to the Lord, asking Him to raise our awareness so we can come against the enemy in victory. Too many students are isolated from their family and from the church. Without godly voices speaking into their young hearts, how will they ever learn to live well? Who will teach them foundational life lessons – truths like how "to possess their own vessel [body] in sanctification and honor, not in passionate of lust like those who do not know God?" (1 Thess. 4:4-5, NAS).

> *The body is not meant for sexual immorality, but for the Lord, and the Lord for the body. Do you not know that your bodies are members of Christ himself?* (1 Cor. 6:13, NAS).

Our Battle is Not Against Flesh and Blood...

As pastors, we have come to realize that an event as mundane as picking up the telephone can often have profound consequences. While walking through our regular morning routine, we received a call from the mother of a teenager. Humbled, she attempted to relay the series of events that lead her to call us. Apparently, a friend of the family agreed to repair her computer, and, in the process, discovered that her 13-year-old son was using it to access a large number of pornographic web sites. The enemy places no restrictions on the age of his targets. Throughout the course of my conversation with her, this mother expressed shock, embarrassment, disappointment, and anger. The underlying theme, however, was guilt and shame. *Why was this happening to her? What had she done wrong? How long had she been deceived? What will she do?*

As we continued to talk together, she confessed that her husband had struggled with pornography for years. While she was aware of his problem, she did not know how to talk to him about it. Helping him to remain in the darkness, she justified his behavior by convincing herself that this particular area of weakness was self-contained. It didn't affect any other area of his life. *Or did it?* She wondered out loud if there was a connection between her husband's struggle and her son's.

In an attempt to determine where this behavior could have originated, she learned that her son discovered his dad's collection of pornographic materials. Unwilling to address the situation with his parents, he never told anyone. Keeping this secret to himself, the sexual images began to consume his mind. Ignoring the guilt inflicted by the illicit photographs that now seemed to control him, he continued to make wrong choices. The trap was set. In an attempt to satisfy the urges that he was unable to control, he typed the word sex into his computer keyboard. The bait was taken.

> *You have heard that it was said, 'Do not commit adultery.'*
> *But I tell you that anyone who looks at a woman lustfully*
> *has already committed adultery with her in his heart* (Matt.
> 5:27, NAS).

Lust is the silent or secret sin. It has been described as a passionate, overmastering desire that eventually seeks to control. Therefore, it is not surprising to hear the number of students who are addicted to pornography increases every day in our user-friendly society. Stories like this one are becoming commonplace. The

Internet is just another tool used to lure a generation away from true intimacy. Since *lust* never satisfies or validates, the victim finds themselves needing more – more sex, more pornography, more food, more money, more power, more whatever.

This endless cycle perpetuates an addictive lifestyle that encourages a counterfeit form of intimacy. The shame and embarrassment that used to be the price one paid in order to purchase illicit sexual materials is now replaced with a false confidence in the anonymity that the Internet provides. The enemy convinces the user that no one will ever find out. His strategy is simple – he wants you to actually believe that you can hide without any personal cost. You can enjoy the benefits of sex without the commitment of a covenantal relationship. Nothing could be further from the truth.

The Enemy's Deluge

An entire generation of students is coming home alone to empty houses each day. Healthy family interaction has subtly been replaced by long hours in front of the TV or on the Internet. The average adolescent will view nearly 14,000 sexual references this year. Over half will contain sexual content. Even the prime time television "family hour" is littered with sexual incidents and innuendoes.

By the time an adolescent graduates from high school, they will have spent 15,000 hours watching television. As far as the Internet, a leading web intelligence and traffic measurement service finds "sex" to be the most popular term searched for online. One in every 300 terms searched for online includes the word sex. People inquire more about sex than they do about games, travel, jokes, cars, jobs, wealth, and health *combined*.[2]

The body is not meant for sexual immorality, but for the Lord, and the Lord for the body...Do you not know that your bodies are members of Christ himself? (1 Cor. 6:13,15 NAS).

God's Redemptive Plan at Work

Sexual promiscuity, rooted in a spirit of lust, continues to inflict the kind of soul-wounding that cries out for deliverance and inner healing. Realizing the value of living in freedom in Christ, we encourage spiritual fathers and mothers to recognize the transforming power connected with discipling the next generation. Ministering freedom to our sexually broken young men and women always starts with God. Seeing His redemptive plan realized in students' lives reminds us that victory over lust is attainable.

As spiritual fathers and mothers, we stand in the gap with parents, resolved to confront lust in whatever form it takes. God's unending grace promises to strengthen the weak and purify the lost.

A student in her mid-twenties walked into our office. Discouraged, she expressed a desire to return home at the semester break. Beginning the school year searching for intimacy with God, she now felt increasingly distant from Him. Unable to measure any evidence of change, she found herself questioning whether or not God's promises would ever be realized in her own life. *What was she doing wrong?* Her quiet times with the Lord felt flat, making them increasingly difficult. Chapel left her uninspired. Obviously something was blocking her from experiencing intimacy with Jesus.

In response, we agreed to meet on a regular basis. The Lord often uses time spent with a young person to give the perspective and understanding needed to identify root issues. In this young lady's case, her childhood was a distorted version of God's family design. At a very young age, she was exposed to her father's pornography addiction. Those images seemed to be permanently imprinted in her mind's eye. At the age of ten, her mother's drug addiction ended in suicide, leaving a void in her life that had not yet been filled. Forced into adulthood, she made an inner vow to guard her heart from the pain of abandonment. In response to her growing need for love and acceptance, she engaged in multiple sexual relationships.

It was in her late teens that she heard the gospel and realized her need for Jesus. Accepting Him as her Lord and Savior was the beginning. She began believing that God had a plan for her life. Over the next few years, she moved around, attending a number of different churches. Her nomadic existence kept her from building stable relationships. Now in her mid-twenties, she found herself sitting in our office at a point of desperation. Tormented by illicit sexual thoughts, she was unable to focus on school or God. The battle left her feeling inadequate and unworthy. *Why is this happening to me? No matter what I do, I can't seem to break free.*

As we met with her over a period of weeks, we began to see His miraculous power at work in her life. We were not just sitting across the table from a student who needed direction or just listening to another story looking for the places to insert some godly counsel. Our time together grew into something much deeper as we began to feel an overwhelming sense of love for her. God's heart toward His daughter was being imparted to us.

As a result, she was able to make a great shift and began moving toward God's best for her.

The Value of Relationship

As we continue to minister to youth, we see God using *relationship* more than anything else as a vehicle for restoration. While deliverance and inner healing are essential to each person's freedom, they often need something more. The loving guidance of a spiritual parent, in conjunction with prayer, fasting, inner healing, and deliverance, often offers the kind of transformation that can be sustained for a lifetime. Young people do not have to have family histories that include broken marriages or severely dysfunctional relationships in order to benefit from the influence a spiritual parent. We all need people in our lives that are willing to walk with us.

It is naïve of us to assume that families offer the kind of environment to their children that facilitates open communication. The young boy who was involved with Internet pornography came from a loving, Christian home. His father, trapped in his own addiction, was unable to offer guidance. His mother admitted to being unable to discuss this sensitive subject with either her husband or her son. Love alone will never be able to equip a child with all that is needed for godly living. This is where the church must rise in an attempt to offer what is lacking.

We see spiritual fathers and mothers not as the answer, but as a vital component of the restoration process. The desire to pray, listen, guide, support, nurture, and love another human being comes from the Father. As we grow in intimacy with Jesus, we are better equipped to impart our lives to the next generation. If discipleship doesn't flow out of our own personal intimacy with Jesus, it will lack substance and authority.

We have come to understand that we cannot take our children further than we have gone ourselves. God's plan for the next generation includes our participation. We have been invited to join Him as He weaves His purposes into a remnant of people who long to live for Him. Delivering our youth into the freedom God intends simply begins with being a part of their life. If we do not give them our time, our energy, our hearts, and our passions, it is for sure that the enemy definitely will.

Notes

[1] "Sexuality, Contraception, and the Media." American Academy of Pediatrics Committee on Public Education. 1/2002.
[2] "Zogby / Focus Survey Reveals Shocking Internet Sex Statistics." Legal Facts: Family Research Council. Vol. 2, No. 20, 3/30/00.

Chapter Five

Freedom from Abortion's Aftermath

John Eckhardt

John Eckhardt is apostle/pastor of Crusaders Ministries in Chicago, Illinois. He has traveled throughout the United States and overseas to over 50 nations imparting biblical truths which include deliverance and spiritual warfare. He has a passion to see the church become truly apostolic by developing the saints for ministry through teaching, training, and demonstration. Apostle Eckhardt produces a daily radio broadcast in the Chicagoland area, and has written many helpful books to assist the body of Christ, including *The Demon Hit List* and *Identifying and Breaking Curses*. These and others of his resources are available by contacting his ministry at (773) 637-2121 or by email at cmimpac@aol.com.

God is raising up women in this hour! He is anointing them prophetically and apostolically to be a strong force for God's Kingdom on earth. God is using deliverance as a tool to release millions of women as ministers of God who can do the works of Jesus Christ; to set them free from curses, generational spirits, from anything that has come upon them. But the truth is that Satan hates women, because it was the seed of a woman that bruised his head (see Gen. 3:15). He is determined to keep women down in such a way that they can never come into the fullness of their true identity. There are certain assignments that demons have against women to keep them oppressed, either as a result of the society that they live in, or because of their decisions. Satan is prevailing in the lives of too many women.

One major tool that Satan has used to accomplish this goal is abortion. The devil has often tricked women into believing that if they have an abortion, their problems will be solved. The enemy will give women all kinds of reasons why abortion is the only answer: they can't financially support their child; the child is going to interrupt their career; or perhaps it's an illegitimate child that will bring shame. The enemy will use any number of means to convince women that having an abortion will make everything okay. But the devil is a liar. Instead of solving all her problems, an abortion works to multiply her problems.

This chapter is directed to those of us who minister deliverance. It is by no means a message meant to condemn any female who has had an abortion. Most women to whom we have ministered, had abortions before they were committed Christians and accepted the Lord Jesus. Abortion is not the unforgivable sin. Nevertheless, we have found that there's a whole system and network of demons that can come in through the door of an abortion, and that can continue to operate in a woman's life long after she is saved. Even though the sin is forgiven by God, Satan's legal right to torment often needs to be dealt with in order for these women to move into all God has for them.

Many years ago in my church, we did an extensive teaching on abortion in which we used Bill Banks' excellent book *Ministering to Abortion's Aftermath* (Impact!) as a textbook, which I highly recommend. We did this teaching because we found that an amazing number of women coming into our church needed deliverance because of one or more abortions. Many of them were under tremendous oppression as a result. I also need to make clear that even though we generally minister to women when it comes to abortion, and that this chapter is written with that perspective in mind, men can be equally involved by encouraging a woman, whether she's his girlfriend, his wife, his daughter, or whatever, to go and have an abortion. When this has occurred, the man is equally guilty of shedding the blood of an innocent child, and he has also opened the door to demonic oppression.

Abortion is such a prevalent sin in America today, that if you are involved in a deliverance ministry, you will likely minister to women who have had abortions and men who have encouraged them. We need to be equipped and understand both the demonic structure behind abortion as well as what the prevailing spirits are that generally oppress those who have been involved in abortion.

The Spirit Behind Abortion

There is no question that God hates the worship of any idol – that's why it is forbidden in the Ten Commandments. But even though there are many, many idols, only a handful of them are mentioned in the Bible. When God specifically mentions a particular idol by name, there must be something about that idol that is especially abominable to God. Behind every idol there is a demon. We know that the idol itself is nothing, but there's a demon force gaining strength from the worship of that idol (see 1 Cor. 10:19-21). Such was the case with one idol named Molech: "And thou shalt not let any of thy seed pass through the fire to Molech, neither shalt thou profane the name of thy God: I am the LORD" (Lev 18:21, KJV).

Later on, God gives a firm warning to those who would involve themselves with Molech: "And the LORD spake unto Moses, saying, 'Again, thou shalt say to the children of Israel, Whosoever he be of the children of Israel, or of the strangers that sojourn in Israel, that giveth any of his seed unto Molech; he shall surely be put to death: the people of the land shall stone him with stones. I will set my face against that man, and will cut him off from among his people; because he hath given of his seed unto Molech, to defile my sanctuary, and to profane my holy name. And if the people of the land do any ways hide their eyes from the man, when he giveth of his seed unto Molech, and kill him not: Then I will set my face against that man, and against his family, and will cut him off, and all that go a whoring after him, to commit whoredom with Molech, from among their people'" (Lev. 20:1-5, KJV).

These Scriptures are not given just to fill up space. There's something about Molech that we need to know which remains true even today.

Who Was Molech?

Molech is a cruel demon spirit who demands its followers' seed, or children, in sacrifice, and has an insatiable desire for innocent blood. Historically, this is an Ammonite spirit. The Ammonites were descendants of Ammon who was one of the sons of Lot whom he had with his own daughter. Molech was the god of the Ammonites, which means that we are not just dealing with a demon, but a principality and it represents a throne of iniquity, as we see in Psalm 94: "Shall the throne of iniquity have fellowship with thee, which frameth mischief by a law? They gather themselves together against the soul of the righteous, and condemn the innocent blood" (vv. 20-21, KJV).

Here we see that the very laws of the Ammonites supported the horrible practices that Molech demanded, including the sacrifice of their sons and daughters. But there was more. In the book of Amos, the prophet is prophesying judgment against different nations for their cruelty toward Israel. He pronounces a particular judgment upon the Ammonites because of something they did. Here is where we see that Molech's desire for innocent blood extends to children still in their mothers' wombs: "Thus saith the LORD; 'For three transgressions of the children of Ammon, and for four, I will not turn away the punishment thereof; because they have ripped up the women with child of Gilead, that they might enlarge their border'" (Amos 1:13, KJV).

God pronounces a judgment against the Ammonites because when they came into a land to conquer it, they had a practice of taking pregnant women and ripping them open to pull the baby out. There must be something demonic that would drive them to do that. I believe that it was Molech, the bloodthirsty god of the Ammonites, that caused them to target women with child. God finally pronounces judgment on them for this grave sin: "'But I will kindle a fire in the wall of Rabbah, and it shall devour the palaces thereof, with shouting in the day of battle, with a tempest in the day of the whirlwind: And their king shall go into captivity, he and his princes together', saith the LORD" (Amos 1:14-15, KJV).

Israel Violates God's Command

Israel violated the commandment of God set forth in Leviticus, and began to get involved with Molech worship. King Solomon was the one who opened the door: "Then did Solomon build an high place for Chemosh, the abomination of Moab, in the hill that is before Jerusalem, and for Molech, the abomination of the children of Ammon" (1 Kings 11:7, KJV).

In Psalm 106, we see how the Lord dealt with Israel for this defiling sin: "And they served their idols: which were a snare unto them. Yea, they sacrificed their sons and their daughters unto devils, And shed innocent blood, even the blood of their sons and of their daughters, whom they sacrificed unto the idols of Canaan: and the land was polluted with blood. Thus were they defiled with their own works, and went a-whoring with their own inventions. Therefore was the wrath of the LORD kindled against his people, insomuch that he abhorred his own inheritance. And he gave them into the hand of the heathen; and they that hated them ruled over them. Their enemies also oppressed them, and they were brought into subjection under their hand" (vv. 36-42, KJV).

As a result of getting involved with sacrificing their children to devils, Israel came under the authority of their enemies to the point of oppression. God had to bring judgment against Israel and to bring them into Babylonian captivity for 70 years because they were fellowshipping with demons.

This was not just an Old Testament problem. First Corinthians has this to say about idolatry and fellowshipping with demons: "Wherefore, my dearly beloved, flee from idolatry. What say I then? That the idol is any thing, or that which is offered in sacrifice to idols is any thing? But I say, that the things which the Gentiles sacrifice, they sacrifice to devils, and not to God: and I would not that ye should have fellowship with devils. Ye cannot drink the cup of the Lord, and the cup of devils: ye cannot be partakers of the Lord's table, and of the table of devils" (1 Cor. 10:14,19-21, KJV).

Molech in Today's World

You may be wondering what all that has to do with abortion today. What we need to realize is that demons and principalities do not die and go to hell. Now, long after the destruction of the Ammonite civilization, the Molech spirit still roams about today to do Satan's bidding. And some things about this evil spirit have not changed. He still craves the blood of innocents. Demons draw strength from blood sacrifices and will work hard for them. Here is where I tie Molech to abortion, because I believe this principality is still manifesting, not necessarily through child sacrifice, but through abortion. Why? Because it is the same thing. When you have an abortion, you are destroying your seed. Abortion is murder, and is the shedding of the most innocent blood of all.

Here in the United States, as in many other nations, Molech gets a lot of blood sacrifices through abortions. Earlier I quoted

Psalm 94, that talks about having fellowship with a throne of iniquity because of the mischief framed by the law, specifically in condemning innocent blood. In other words, a law can be passed that actually promotes something that God hates. One of the things demons try to do is to get involved with legal systems in order to pass laws that build thrones of iniquity in that society.

I believe this passage in Psalm 94 is a good description of the whole problem of abortion. Abortion has been approved by law in this nation, just as the Ammonites legally approved the sacrificing of their children – condemning innocent blood. And the thing behind it, both then and today, is a throne of iniquity tied to Molech. There are millions of babies who have been aborted since abortion was legalized. It has opened the door for incredible amounts of oppression and demonization for those involved. Why? Because when an individual commits an act that is tied in with a demonic structure, they open the door for that demonic structure to activate in their own lives. Abortion, therefore, is not just a harmless little sin that you can get away with. It actually connects that person with the particular spirits behind it, which will inevitably affect them, their generations, and open them to all kinds of curses.

Judgments on Those
Who Shed Innocent Blood

Now that we see how abortion is tied in with Molech, it is important to go back and see the judgments that came upon those who shed innocent blood. As we have ministered to countless women over this issue, we have seen that many of these same judgments are operating in their lives. The following is not meant to be a pat formula, but is meant to offer an understanding of why certain spirits can activate in the lives of those involved in abortion.

The first several spirits that we have found operating in cases of abortion can be found in Jeremiah 32:35-36: "And they built the high places of Baal, which are in the valley of the son of Hinnom, to cause their sons and their daughters to pass through the fire unto Molech; which I commanded them not, neither came it into my mind, that they should do this abomination, to cause Judah to sin. And now therefore thus saith the LORD, the God of Israel, concerning this city, whereof ye say, 'It shall be delivered into the hand of the king of Babylon by the sword, and by the famine, and by the pestilence'" (KJV).

Spirit of Death

In this verse we see three judgments the Lord imposed on those who shed innocent blood as sacrifice to Molech. The first was the sword, which represents death. This is tied in strongly with a spirit of hell, which I explain further down.

Spirit of Poverty

The second judgment was famine, which represents poverty. Women who have had abortions will many times (although not always) have trouble in their finances. Even if that is not the specific problem they tend to have a famine of some kind in their lives, whether it's with their careers or finances or certain relationships. *Sometimes the very thing they were trying to save by not having the baby is the very thing that comes under the attack of the devil.* Cain was the first one in the Bible to shed innocent blood. To understand this idea of famine and poverty better, let's look at the judgment that came upon him as a result of killing his brother: "And he said, 'What hast thou done? the voice of thy brother's blood crieth unto me from the ground. And now art thou cursed from the earth, which hath opened her mouth to receive thy brother's blood from thy hand; When thou tillest the ground, it shall not henceforth yield unto thee her strength; a fugitive and a vagabond shalt thou be in the earth'" (Gen. 4:10-12, KJV).

This curse represents the assignment of a spirit of poverty. No matter how hard someone with a spirit of poverty works or how much seed they put into the ground, the ground never gives back its full strength. One of the first curses that can come upon a person who sheds innocent blood is that the earth does not cooperate with you. All the prosperity that God put on this planet comes from the earth. The gold, silver, agriculture, oil – all of it comes out of the earth. When the earth does not yield its strength, there is not prosperity. We need the earth to cooperate with us. The earth is the Lord's and all the fullness thereof. As we break these curses and do deliverance, the earth will begin to release its blessings.

Spirit of Sickness and Infirmity

The third curse we find in Jeremiah 32 is pestilence, which represents sickness and disease. We have found that many women opened the door for strong spirits of sickness and infirmity to come in through abortion. Again, this varies from female to female. Some females have abortions and their life seems to be better, while others have abortions and their life seems to fall apart. It will obviously depend on who you are praying for.

Spirit of Hell

In the Jeremiah 32 passage quoted above, notice that Molech worship was established in the valley of the son of Hinnom, which was a valley outside of Jerusalem. That's very important because the valley of Hinnom in the Hebrew was translated as Gehenna in Greek, which represented hell. Jesus used Gehenna to typify hell several times as He warned against the consequences of sin (see Matt.

5:22,29-30; 10:28; 18:9; 23:15,33; Mark 9:43,45,47; Luke 12:5). He described it as a place where their worm never dies and their fire. This was literally true, because after Josiah destroyed this idol in the valley of Hinnom (Gehenna), it became a garbage dump where fire was always burning and where the worm never died. This place called hell was tied into the worship of Molech.

But hell is not just a place, hell is also a spirit. There's a demon called hell. Death is not just an event, there's a spirit called death. I believe that also attached to the spirits of Molech and abortion are spirits of death and hell, which are two major end-

Thank God that Jesus came that those who have had abortions might be set free!

time principalities found in Revelation 6:8: "And I looked, and behold a pale horse: and his name that sat on him was Death, and Hell followed with him. And power was given unto them over the fourth part of the earth, to kill with sword, and with hunger, and with death, and with the beasts of the earth" (NIV).

People who involve themselves with abortions can have a spirit of hell in their life. They may say, "My life is hell." The spirit of hell's job is to torment people and make their life so miserable that it becomes like a living hell on earth. Hell is a place of torment – no rest, no peace. Death works with hell. Those afflicted by these spirits are not even dead yet, but there's something in them that makes them feel that they're not living. Jesus said, "I come that you might have life and that you might have it more abundantly." The spirits of death and hell in a person will keep them from enjoying the abundant life that Jesus provided. But I believe we don't have to have hell on earth. I believe we can have heaven on earth. I believe we can have the glory of God on earth. I believe we can have the liberty and the joy and the peace of God. As opposed to hell, heaven is a place of peace. Thank God for deliverance!

Vagabond and Fugitive Spirits

Another lesson we learn from the curse on Cain is that those who shed innocent blood are subject to vagabond and fugitive spirits (see Gen. 4:12). A vagabond is one who can never find a resting place. A vagabond spirit manifests in a life by causing the person to not be able to settle down into one relationship, one job, one city, one church, and so on. They don't make meaningful commitments. No one can prosper always running, hiding, dodging, and not getting their roots established. This is a wandering spirit that works much like the poverty spirit.

A fugitive spirit causes people to live in fear, just trying to stay alive. Sometimes women with this spirit end up in abusive relationships. Other times they are tormented. They have no peace or rest and feel as if something is after them. They often can't sleep and exist in fear and darkness. Proverbs 28:1 says, "The wicked flee when no one pursues" (KJV).

This is a good description of someone afflicted by a fugitive spirit. But God did not put us on the earth just to stay alive, but to have the abundant life that Jesus provides. That's why deliverance is so important.

The Rachel Spirit

Another spirit we have had to deliver many women from is called Rachel. This comes from Matthew 2:18: "A voice was heard in Ramah, lamentation, weeping, and great mourning, Rachel weeping for her children, refusing to be comforted, because they are no more" (KJV). This passage refers to the time when Herod had all the children two and under murdered in an attempt to kill Jesus. Rachel represents women that weep because of the loss of their children. Many times when we cast this spirit out of women, even if the loss of her child was due to an abortion, there is a wail that comes out of them that sounds like a woman that has just lost her child. There is no sound that can be compared to a woman that has just lost her child. There's a spirit of weeping, sadness, grief, hurt— all of these spirits can operate in women who have had abortions. Because whether we realize it or not, women were not emotionally made to deal with the abortion of a child. Of course, there can come a time when the conscience is seared, but that is not natural. More often, there is a profound grief and sadness that comes.

The natural cycle of childbirth is to go through pregnancy and then go through travail. But then after the travail the Bible says that for the joy of having that child, the woman forgets her travail. That is the natural process. Once you hold that child there is a joy that comes. But when a woman does not go through that process, she never experiences the joy. The process is short-circuited, and there is a grief and a travail and a sadness and a heaviness and a depression that is never overcome by actually having the baby. It's almost as if they are in perpetual travail.

This can also happen to women who have had miscarriages or stillbirths. We have had to cast out grief, sadness, travail, and the spirit of refusing to be comforted. Rachel refused to be comforted. This spirit can actually hinder a woman from receiving the comfort of the Lord. God can't comfort you if you don't let Him. As a side note, when we cast out a Rachel spirit, we are not talking about the actual Rachel of the Bible. She is in heaven. We are talking about demons that are identified with this type of weeping, lamenting, hurting, travailing, grieving, and those spirits often lodge in the emotional area. As a result, we often have to deal with oppression, depression, discouragement, sadness, and hopelessness as well.

The Prayer Process

No one can abort a baby and expect their life to be okay. It's the law of sowing and reaping. It opens the door for all kinds of tragedy and death, and demonic cycles such as those I've just described. This is a major issue in the heart of God. I've seen women who've had abortion and the man is gone, but they are still struggling and can't get ahead. Jesus is the answer. He will forgive them. He will deliver them. He will drive those curses and spirits out of their life.

But in order to get there, she will need ministry. When you're praying for a woman who has told you of an abortion, you need to first get her to repent for having the abortion and ask God's forgiveness covered with the blood. Second, break any curses of murder, death, destruction, poverty, or sickness that may have come as a result of the abortion. Third begin to call the spirits out that came in through the door of abortion as listed above and any others that the Holy Spirit may show you.

Many times you will then see a great release and that woman's life will turn completely around. She will be a new woman. God wants to prosper that woman; He wants to bless that woman; He does not want that woman to live a hard, difficult, travailing life. Thank God for deliverance! Thank God that Jesus came that those who have had abortions, and indeed all we who have ever sinned, might be set free!

Chapter Six

Freedom from Homosexual Confusion

David Kyle Foster

David is the author of *Sexual Healing: God's Plan for the Sanctification of Broken Lives*, and *Transformed Into His Image*. He has served as adjunct professor at Asbury Theological Seminary, The Bible Institute of Hawaii, Trinity Episcopal School for Ministry, Logos Christian College & Graduate School, and is on the faculty of the Wagner Leadership Institute. His articles have appeared in numerous Christian journals and magazines and he has been on countless television and radio programs, Christian and secular, witnessing to God's healing of sin and brokenness. David is the founder and director of Mastering Life Ministries and serves as a "Canon" at Church of the Messiah in Jacksonville, Florida. You can contact David's ministry online at www.MasteringLife.org or by calling 904-220-7474.

Freedom from the Lies

Jesus made it clear that Satan is "a liar and the father of lies" (Jn. 8:44, NIV). Because God only blesses faith, the strategy of the evil one has been to gain power by inciting unbelief. Therefore, a significant part of being freed from the power of sin comes in ferreting out the lies that we have believed, renouncing them, and aggressively embracing the truth as revealed by God. For God declares in His Word that it is "the knowledge of the truth that leads to godliness" (Titus 1:1, NIV).

Lie # 1 - The Bible does not condemn homosexual acts.

In reality, homosexuals do not exist. You will not find the word in Scripture or in any other writing before the 19th century. What you find in the Bible are descriptions of same-sex *behaviors* and condemnation for those who engage in them (e.g., Lv. 18:22; 20:13; Rom. 1:25-27; 1 Cor. 6:9).

These biblical descriptions are very clear (despite modern attempts to make them appear ambiguous). For example, the Hebrew word for a male "lying with a male" used in Leviticus 18:22 and 20:13, *mishkav zakur*, was translated into Greek in the

Septuagint as *arsenos koiten*. The apostle Paul takes those very words and coins a new word, *arsenokoitai*, in 1 Corinthians 6:9 when stating that those who commit homosexual acts will not inherit the kingdom of God. There is no doubt that by his word choice, Paul is declaring that the Torah prohibition of homosexual behavior is part of the unchangeable moral law rather than a part of the ritual/ceremonial law that was fulfilled by Christ.

Romans 1 is also very clear in its description and condemnation of homosexual acts as being rebellion against God and a part of the disordered human condition. Those who claim otherwise break cardinal rules of interpretation and presume to know better than all of the expert Bible scholar-translators who have ever lived in the 2000 plus years of Bible translation.

Lie # 2 - The field of psychology has proven that homosexuals are born that way.

In press releases and public debates, modern gay activism likes to give the impression that the field of psychology has proven that homosexuality is healthy and normal, and the claim that it is disordered is a new and dangerous theory held by those who do not know what they are talking about. In truth, if one looks at the thought, research, and reported experience of psychologists and other professional counselors throughout history, the novel theory with no basis in reality is the gay activist one.

As the field of psychology emerged more than 100 years ago, it's practitioners began to organize human *behaviors* into categories, labeling them as an aid to study and diagnosis. Unfortunately, in our day the artificial construct known as "homosexual" has been misconstrued as a true and inherent identity, something a person is born with; something, therefore, that cannot change. It's as if the word rose up from the page and became the thing itself.

This morphing of terminology did not come about as a result of scientific research and study, but as a consequence of pressure from gay activist groups who threw tantrums and made threats at various professional association meetings in the 1970s, and who have skillfully infiltrated and manipulated media coverage of the issue ever since. (I recommend Dr. Jeffrey Satinover's brilliant book, *Homosexuality and the Politics of Truth* [Baker Books] for a detailed, eyewitness account of how this happened.)

Study after study has failed to show a genetic or other physiological cause for homosexual neurosis. In fact, several have shown just the opposite. At least two studies that were purported to prove a genetic cause for homosexual orientation (the *"Hamer"* and the "identical twin" studies) actually proved that the orientation could *not* be determined by genetics. The "identical twin" study, for example, found discordant sets of *genetically identical* twins (where one was gay and the other straight) an impossible outcome if homosexuality is caused by genetics.

Lie # 3 - Homosexuality is fixed and unchangeable.

A few years ago, Dr. Robert Spitzer, one of the men most responsible for caving in to gay activist pressure at American Psychiatric Association (APA) meetings in the early 1970s (when they removed homosexuality from their official list of disorders) decided to conduct an actual study of homosexuals. He found to his surprise that people with this struggle were *not* hopelessly fixed in their orientation and that many could and have changed. As a result, those who earlier considered Dr. Spitzer to be the darling of the gay movement, now vilify him because he dared to ground his professional opinion in scientific research and to publicly reveal what he had found.

It is critical that we understand the mistake that our culture has made in this matter. Why? Because people generally believe that an *inherent identity* is impossible to change and confers acceptance for its exercise on the one so afflicted. This semantic sleight of hand has provided an excuse for many to yield to unholy desire and most people who have been misled by it aren't even aware of the ruse.

In addition, there is formative power in a name. People tend to become the label that has been given them by authority figures. The more identified a person becomes with the name "homosexual," the more difficult it will be for that person to see him- or herself as anything else. This factor alone can make one person's transformation take much longer than another's once they've entered into the process of healing and change.

Lie # 4 - Homosexuality is healthy and normal.

Gay activism and its mouthpiece, the liberal media, claim that homosexuals are just as happy and healthy as the rest of us (an actual statement in one of their newspaper ads). Once again, nothing could be further from the truth! According to Dr. Jeffrey Satinover, maladies that plague those who participate in homosexual behavior include: chronic, potentially fatal, liver disease (hepatitis) which often leads to cancer; fatal immune disease (AIDS); frequently fatal rectal cancer; multiple bowel and other infectious diseases; a much higher rate of suicide; and a 25-30 year decrease in life expectancy. You could add to that astronomical rates of alcoholism, drug addiction, and (particularly among lesbians) domestic violence.

It is clear that homosexuals are internally driven to self-destructive behavior as a result of the lies that they have believed about themselves, about God, and about the purpose of life. Any plan to help them find freedom must deal with the deceptions that the enemy has sown in their hearts and minds. If such lies can be broken and replaced by the truth found only in Jesus Christ, then the destructive power of their bondage can be broken as well.

Freedom from the Brokenness

Other than lies, what else does the person who suffers from homosexual confusion need to be delivered from? Is it a disease that God can instantly heal? Is the condition itself sin, that merely requires genuine repentance? Or is it a demon that, when successfully cast out, takes with it the orientation?

None of the above. It is true that upon repentance some experience such an infusion of God's life and power that it seems as though He has supernaturally removed the brokenness altogether. As time goes on, however, it becomes clear that there is still much that remains to be healed.

It is disappointing to learn at first, but a glorious truth nonetheless, that being transformed into the image of Christ is not achieved by having our susceptibility to temptation supernaturally removed, but by deepening our love for God so that in the midst of such temptation we freely and joyfully choose Him rather than our former idols.

Jesus was tempted in the wilderness and tempted in the Garden – yet without sin. It is into that likeness that we are being formed. Without the temptation, there is nothing to spur growth, nothing to test righteousness, no opportunity to be like Christ.

The transformation process includes great moments of revelation and deliverance interspersed with long roads of hard growth and struggle. There are peaks and valleys, joys and sorrows, times when you feel in perfect union with God and His holiness and times when you feel as though He has vanished and cast you into the hands of your former gods. Such are the deep waters where faith is born, seemingly empty places where God is never so close, yet feels ever so far.

The Cause

God creates us to be heterosexual. We are naturally designed to go in male-female pairs. However, at birth our sexuality is in seed form, a kind of time-released seed that is designed to lie dormant for a number of years, and finally germinate and flower during the years of puberty. Though dormant in the early years, the seed needs to be protected and requires proper nurture in order to germinate properly at the appointed time. In those who develop homosexual confusion during their formative years, that seed either gets damaged or fails to receive the nutrients that it needs to germinate properly. What arises in its place is a false identity derived from ill-conceived attempts to jerry-rig an identity where none exists.

Homosexual confusion, neurosis, orientation—whatever you want to call it—is a form of arrested emotional development that in its early stages is caused by a constellation of environmental factors (usually involving trauma and neglect). These factors negatively affect the sexual identity development of those whose temperament and surroundings make them uniquely susceptible to such influences. This blend of factors interacts and conspires with the temperament, character and personality traits of the individual as cogs do in a wheel.

This would explain why so many in the gay community are found to have a highly sensitive temperament. These are folks who feel the impact of the traumas and neglects of life more deeply and are broken by them more easily. Their "seed" has been either damaged or improperly fed. Those so afflicted, often find themselves saddled with feelings of being different or inadequate, and suffer an ambiguous sense of incompleteness as males or females.

This results in a longing to be made one with their estranged gender.

In an attempt to heal (or complete) themselves, such people often make wrong choices and thus become co-conspirators in the worsening of their broken condition. They fix on the creature rather than the Creator as a source of hope and identity, thus, unwittingly at first, making idols of those who seem to epitomize the ideal man or woman. The incredibly powerful force of sexual awakening (whether at puberty, or prematurely via pornography or while being sexually abused), then distorts what is at its root an emotional need, causing it to be perceived as sexual. If they continue to ride this snowball of lust and idolatry, then the demonic realm gains the foothold it needs to create a stronghold, compounding the problem even further.

The most common factor found in males is a failure to emotionally bond or identify with a father-figure. (Any number of scenarios could illustrate why this might happen, such as an environment where dad is absent, abusive, emotionally weak, or distant; where the feminine influence is stronger or where the mother-figure continually communicates disfavor of men or things masculine.) Without the approval, affirmation, and modeling of a father-figure who can draw them into fixing their identity in masculinity (this could be someone other than the father, such as a scoutmaster, a coach, even an older brother), some preteen boys will remain identified with the feminine (which happened at birth, when they naturally bonded with their mother). Much of the effeminate tendencies can be explained by this failure to switch identity from mom to dad during a boy's early years.

Females sometimes fail to emotionally bond with their mothers, which can be a core factor in the development of lesbian tendencies, although this is not as common as it is in males. In females, by far the most common factor is childhood sexual abuse. Some figures suggest that as high as 85% of all lesbians have been victims of childhood sexual abuse. It's easy to see how such a traumatic event might cause some girls to develop an identity-dominating aversion to the gender of their perpetrator.

What makes the difference between those who develop homosexual tendencies as a result of being sexually abused and those who do not? Once again we need to look at variables such as: temperament, spiritual and emotional health, a safe and healing environment, the kind of abuse, the age of being abused, the number of times, the severity, etc. In any given girl, any number of variables might mitigate the outcome.

Childhood sexual abuse is also prevalent in the backgrounds of male homosexuals, making it the second most common causal factor for them. Some figures suggest that at least half of all males with homosexual orientation have suffered sexual abuse as children or adolescents. The odd difference with males is that many of them do not see their own sexual abuse as abuse, but as being the only source of attention that anyone ever gave them. Thus, many abused males will not admit to being victims. Girls, on the other hand, are much more likely to see their abuse as a violation of their person.

Space does not allow us to discuss many of the other factors that can play into the development of sexual identity confusion. For example, family dynamics can sometimes play a powerful role, such as when a mother gives birth to a baby whose gender is opposite from what mom and/or dad wanted and the child only receives love, attention and affirmation when they behave and identify with the opposite gender. This can be profoundly confusing and formative for a sensitive child.

In short, homosexual confusion is usually innocently acquired, but then made worse by the sinful reactions of those so afflicted. As they move into idolatry, whether out of lust or an attempt to heal themselves, God eventually gives them over to the idols that they choose (Ez. 16:39; Rom. 1:24). At this point, they can only be brought back to God through repentance and a dogged determina-

God Himself replaces the former idols and becomes the hope, the life, and the love of that person.

tion to follow the Holy Spirit as He leads them through multiple layers of repentance, healing, and transformation.

In that process, God exposes and (as the person becomes willing) breaks the demonic stronghold of lies that has given power to sinful desire and the root sin of unbelief. God Himself replaces the former idols and becomes the hope, the life, and the love of that person. As that relationship deepens, "the things of earth grow strangely dim, in the light of His glory and grace" (from the song, "Turn Your Eyes Upon Jesus").

The Cure

"Deliverance" for those who suffer from same-sex attraction is first and foremost a matter of being set free from the lies that they were born that way, that God cannot change them, and that they are excused from the biblical prohibitions of same-sex behavior by some fated condition.

When people renounce and forsake the lies and the false gods that they have used as a means to personal fulfillment or development, the healing begins. As they turn to God to be their source and primary love, He begins to unveil the roots of fallen desire and leads them through a process of transformation. It is critical that whatever other counselors God may use to help them along the way, that the Holy Spirit become their primary Counselor.

Deliverance for a person who struggles with same-sex attraction can be a lengthy process, depending on their willingness to do whatever it takes, their depth of love for God above all others, the passion in their pursuit of Him, their age, the length and depth of their involvement in the sins associated with the condition, and other such variables.

There may be demons that have taken advantage of the person's sin and become a part of the problem, but there is no "demon of homosexuality" that has been the sole cause of this condition. Each person developed homosexual desire through a unique and complex matrix of elements that must be uncovered and dealt with in an appropriate fashion. As with many other life-dominating bondages, some of the more common elements include: idolatry, rebellion, anger, unforgiveness, unbelief, love of sin, a skewed image of God, self-centeredness, performance-orientation, self-hatred, fear, etc. The Holy Spirit knows exactly what the mix is for each individual, the timing and order in which each need to be addressed, and the salutary replacements that need to be imparted. He also has all power in heaven and earth at His disposal.

In some ways, the process of getting free from same-sex attraction is like the process of salvation. It is three-tiered and multifaceted. Of salvation, the Bible is clear that we are saved (Acts 15:11; 1 Cor. 15:2; Eph. 2:5,8; Titus 3:5), we are being saved (1 Cor 1:18), and we will be saved (Mt. 24:13; Mk. 13:13). Of this, Dr. John R. W. Stott has written: "Salvation is a good word; it denotes that comprehensive purpose of God by which he justifies, sanctifies, and glorifies his people: first pardoning their offenses and accepting them as righteous in his sight; then progressively transforming them by his Spirit into the image of Christ, until finally they become like Christ in heaven, when they see him as he is, and their bodies are raised incorruptible like Christ's body of glory. I long to rescue salvation from the narrow concepts to which even evangelical Christians sometimes reduce it." [1]

In a similar way, the healing of homosexual orientation is a three-tiered process. Homosexuals receive a degree or dimension of deliverance when they repent and give their life to Christ. Even so, as the Holy Spirit continues to unveil the secret roots of their condition, they continue to be delivered to a greater and greater degree. Then, on that last day when Christ appears and transforms them into His image completely, they will be delivered fully and for all time.

If God were to instantly zap them free from being homosexually-oriented, they would be free from that particular kind of temptation, but would still be the same immature and broken people as before. Instead, God leads them through a measured and deliberate process of discovering the wrong choices they have made, why they made them, and offers them an opportunity to willfully forsake those choices, one by one. In essence, He teaches them how to love (defined in 1 Jn. 3:16; 3:18 as "sacrifice" and "commitment"), and He does so in the midst of trial so that their choice to love is hard-won, substantive and thus, meaningful.

Freedom – A Personal Story

To illustrate, allow me to recount for you parts of my own journey of healing from homosexual confusion. When I got saved at the age of twenty-nine, I had been suffering from homosexual confusion most of my life and had been continuously active in the lifestyle for over ten years. I was hopelessly out of control and was convinced that if God didn't set me free by some supernatural means, it would never happen.

The first thing that God did was to send a great grace upon me that enabled me to recognize the evil that I had embraced, so that I could repent from the heart (1 Jn. 1:9). I finally knew that I was a sinner and desperately in need of God's grace.

Upon repenting, God swept into my very being, bringing with Him the power to resist what had previously been irresistible temptation (Mt. 3:11; Jn. 4:10; 7:37-38). It was a great delivering moment that came as I prayed in my room for Him to set me free. I had read in Matthew 5:6 that if I hungered and thirsted for righteousness, He would fill me with it, and He did. Make no mistake, I was still fully capable of committing the same sinful acts as before, and at times mightily tempted to do so, but after praying Matthew 5:6 with all my heart, God removed the coercive power that the demonic realm held over me as a result of my wicked ways, and I was able to freely choose between good and evil for the first time in a long time.

Next, He gave me an awareness that there were demonic spirits that needed casting out. Being alone and too afraid of trusting the church down the street with the knowledge of my sins, I somehow knew that I could cast them out myself. By then, I was fully aware of God's great power over Satan and my new authority as a child of God to call on that power for such a task (Lk. 10:19; Jn. 14:12-14). And I was thoroughly persuaded never to return to that sinful lifestyle. So the Lord led me to call the evil spirits by name (according to what they were tempting me to do), and I commanded them to leave me and the place where I was staying in the name of Jesus. Within a week, they were completely gone.

The Lord also gave me revelation as to how my healing was going to come to pass. I was to concentrate on falling in love with Him at deeper and deeper levels and He was going to reveal and empower everything else that was needed. Through some timely advice from a pastor, God enabled me to see that the battle was the Lord's (1 Sam. 17:47; Ez. 36:25-27). It was going to be His power released on my behalf that would keep me free from bondage (Jude 24), and that my job was to get into His presence so that I could be led by the Spirit (Gal. 5:16). In His presence would come the infilling of the Holy Spirit by which the desire to be holy would be replenished. In His presence would be where my yearning to co-operate with Him through the difficult times would be renewed.

God said in His Word that "His divine power has given us everything we need for life and godliness *through our knowledge of him*" (2 Pet. 1:3, NIV, emphasis added). It has been through that knowledge, that intimacy, that God has delivered me and kept me from falling, because His beauty and the pleasure of His company far surpasses that of all gods.

In coming to know Him more deeply through the revelation of His love demonstrated on the Cross, I have been persuaded that He is worthy to be obeyed and can be trusted. In meditating on the Cross that He bore and in experiencing the crosses that He has asked me to bear, I have come to know Him in the fellowship of His sufferings (Phil. 3:10; Rom. 8:17; 1 Pet. 4:13).

In the revelation of His grace, as He forgives me again and again and again, my heart has been transformed and knit to His (Titus 2:11-14). I no longer see Him as an adversary. I see Him as love. And that revelation has struck a mighty blow against the rebellion that used to reign in my heart. He has taught me how to starve the old man and feed the new. And He has transformed my inner motivation for doing so from duty to love.

In intimate moments with the Lord, I often sing love songs to Him and He sometimes responds with life-changing revelation, healing words of love, visions of glory, or infusions of divine life and power (2 Pet. 1:4). As I focus on loving Him, He imparts His very nature (2 Cor. 3:18).

Sometimes He reminds me of a particular incident and a person that I need to forgive. At other times, He exposes love for a sin that lingers in the dark inner reaches of my heart, so that I can renounce it. And sometimes, He seems to vanish and leave me without any consolation or assurance that He loves me or that He even exists. Yet even those moments are acts of love, designed for my growth in Christ-likeness, for it is when we love and obey Him, even when His hand of provision and blessing has been removed, that we grow to be most like Him. For that is also a part of the nature of Christ, as He demonstrated in the Garden of Gethsemane when all seemed lost and forsaken.

Over the years, God has led me to unite with various fellowships and small groups of Christians where I could learn to know and be known as I truly am. He has sent me to life-changing conferences and arranged other divine appointments with those who had just the right word, hug, or blessing.

He has put me in places where I could get prayer to break the soul ties that were formed with former sexual partners as well as prayer to break family-line curses (Num. 14:18; Ez. 18:14-17). He has enabled me to forgive people who I didn't think I could ever forgive. He has shown me how to love, how to serve and sacrifice for others.

God has also imparted to me a mature sense of masculinity, which had always been missing. He has spoken words of love and sonship into my spirit that have healed deep inner wounds and insecurities. He has given me a healthy view of men and removed my fear of women, enabling me to see them as the glorious creatures that they are.

He has taught me how to rejoice in my weaknesses and to use them as a reminder of my absolute dependence on Him (2 Cor. 12:9-10). I now enjoy staying under the shelter of His Almighty hand. God has imparted to me, (through many trials and testings), a capacity to trust and obey Him that is far beyond all that I could have ever imagined. He has healed my desperate sadness and broken spirit and filled me with divine life (Is. 61). He has renewed my mind (Eph. 4:23; Rom. 12:2) and shown me how to guard it (Phil. 4:7). He has replaced what I lost and healed what I damaged (Joel 2:25).

He has taught me the schemes of the enemy and the greater strategies that heaven has devised to overcome them (Eph. 6:10-18). He has taught me how to put to death that which feeds the old broken self (Rom. 8:13-14), and how to feed and nurture the new creation that I have been made by Christ (2 Cor. 5:17; Eph. 4:24). In doing so, the heterosexuality that had always lain dormant within me was finally able to blossom and take its place as my true identity. And in those moments when my mind slips back into the old ways of feeling and thinking, He whispers words of love in my spirit and I run back into His arms and embrace anew the miracle that is Christ in me (Gal. 2:20; Col. 1:27).

Can a person who has struggled with homosexual orientation be delivered and set free from that bondage to lust and idolatry? Well, is the Pope Catholic?

Notes

[1] Dr. John R. W. Stott, *Authentic Christianity* (Downer's Grove, IL, InterVarsity Press), p. 169.

Chapter Seven

Child Sexual Abuse

Tom R. Hawkins

Tom, Founder and President of Restoration in Christ Ministries, has helped hundreds of sexual abuse victims since the 1980s. He specializes in those who also experienced Ritual Abuse and mind-control programming and have developed Dissociative Identity Disorder as a result. With a Ph.D. in Biblical Studies, he claims no mental health credentials. However, from 1991 to 1993, he worked closely with mental health professionals in one of the few Christian in-patient Dissociative Disorders Units in the United States. He is joined by his wife, Diane, in a prolific seminar ministry. To contact his ministry, please write Restoration in Christ Ministries, PO Box 479,Grottoes, VA 24441-0479, phone 540-249-9119, or e-mail rcm@rcm-usa.org. The website is www.rcm-usa.org.

Diane was born into a Christian home, made a personal commitment to Christ at age six, and graduated from high school and college at the top of her class. Considered brilliant and spiritually committed, she completed her Masters degree in Christian Ministries, went on to become a missionary, and eventually married at age 30.

Within a year of marrying, however, her life began to unravel. Only after seven years of an intense search for answers in the medical and mental health community did she begin to understand the reason for her emotional turmoil and the extensive gaps in her childhood memories. Evidence of overwhelming trauma that her child psyche had been unable to cope with began to surface, including child sexual abuse.

Her story is neither unique nor unusual, as child sexual abuse affects the lives of millions of men and women around the world. While using a host of psychological defense mechanisms to cope with it, these children usually grow up to experience significant pain, dysfunction, and misery in their adult lives. These profound and long-lasting effects impact their families, churches, and communities as well.

Biblical View of the Sexual Relationship

Child sexual abuse needs to be understood and addressed from the perspective of the biblical framework that God established for the human sexual relationship. His unequivocal standard is for sex to occur only between one adult man and one adult woman in a life-long, monogamous, covenant union. Most Christians believe that God intends us to have this kind of sexual union for both pleasure and procreation (Gen. 2:24-25). Any kind of sexual relationship outside of these strictly-defined boundaries is, for our own well-being, strictly prohibited (1 Cor. 6:12-20).

God's powerful admonitions against sexual activity occurring outside of marriage by implication cover any sexual contact what-soever with children (Matt. 18:6). When adults exchange "the natural use for what is against nature…to do those things which are not fitting…" (Rom. 1:26,28), negative consequences are inevitable.

Understanding God's joyous view of the sexual relationship within marriage is an important part of childhood development. However, children should be protected from exposure to sexual activity and stimulation. Children, being physically and emotion-ally immature, are greatly confused when thrust into the dynamics of a sexual relationship or any intrusive sexual exposure.

Defining Child Sexual Abuse

Child sexual abuse involves any kind of sexual contact or exploita-tion of a minor for the sexual stimulation of the perpetrator. Fon-dling (touch of any area normally covered by a "decent" bathing suit); inappropriate kissing; and oral, genital, or anal penetration all involve physical contact with the child. However, directing inappropriate comments with sexual innuendoes at a child or exposing a child to pornographic material or to any inappropriate exhibition of sexual organs or sexual activity between adults is also considered child sexual abuse. All such behaviors are generally considered criminal behavior.[1]

Sadly, the secular media and the Internet have contributed to creating a society in which sexual dynamics are exploited and made public in a very unhealthy way, manipulating adults into immoral behavior and exposing children to what they are psychologically and emotionally not ready to handle. Kinsey and his fabricated "studies" have also contributed greatly to the societal distortion of the biblical ideal.[2]

It is estimated that approximately two million children each year are abused.[3] Conservative estimates indicate that a large number of them are being sexually abused. Many such cases are unreported.[4] Numerous statistical studies indicate that 20 to 40 percent of females[5] and up to 25 percent of males will have been sexually abused by the age of 18. In the majority of cases the children are abused by someone they know and trust. Victims can be found among every social, racial, economic, and religious group.

The Pervasive Effects of Child Sexual Abuse

Sadly, the physical, emotional, psychological, and spiritual effects of child sexual abuse are devastating in their impact, even if the abuse does not include "penetration" of a body opening or occurs only once. I do not agree with the notion that these effects occur only as the result of a repressive, "puritanical" upbringing. I believe the multi-faceted impact on a child is much more than a sociological phenomenon; it is the natural consequence of violating God's creative order. Each case is unique, however, as not all children evidence the same long-term consequences.[6]

Many specific symptoms have been documented, and lists can easily be found by searching the relevant literature. A child's self-concept and worldview are often significantly distorted when the sanctity of their bodies is violated. When children are manipulated with lies or misrepresentations about moral standards, their sense of morality is understandably affected at a deep level as well. When the abuse occurs at the hand of a significant caregiver, the child feels an overwhelming sense of betrayal. This sense of betrayal is compounded if they try to disclose their abuse and are disbelieved, blamed, or ostracized. Intense distrust of adults may occur and manifest in the form of angry outbursts or isolation and avoidance of close relationships. Another almost universal effect of child sexual abuse is the sense of powerlessness or "disempowerment" the child feels.[7]

The invasion of a child's body and "personal space" against their will commonly affects their ability to establish and maintain proper boundaries throughout life. Exaggerated fears (phobias) are also common. In fact, nearly all of the negative emotions can be problematic in a sexual abuse victim's life if they are not properly addressed. Psychosomatic physical symptoms can also result and prevail throughout the individual's life, especially when the child copes by dissociating or repressing the event and its emotions.

David Finkelhor and Angela Browne have documented that sexual feelings and attitudes may be developmentally shaped in a dysfunctional manner for a victim of child sexual abuse.[8] Abused children become confused about their sexuality and later, as adults, are often unable to function healthily within a marriage relationship. Their dysfunctional symptoms can range from hatred of their body and avoidance of sex, on the one hand, to compulsive and inappropriate sexual behaviors/promiscuity on the other.

Bessel van der Kolk has written widely about the inability of many such victims to regulate their emotions properly, resulting in depression and low self-esteem coupled with outbursts of anger.[9] This anger may seem inappropriate or out of proportion to the present situation, but it is triggered when the individual encounters or experiences something that consciously or unconsciously reminds them of the abusive events in the past.

The difference in how males and females handle the inevitable anger they feel over being wronged and violated is noteworthy. There are always exceptions to every rule. However, males are generally more apt to "act out" with their anger, while females tend to turn their anger inward onto themselves. Consequently, sexually abused males often end up in the legal and judicial system, while females are more apt to seek help through social services institutions, the mental health field, or prayer ministries for the resulting depression and poor self-image.

Females are also more apt to engage in eating disorders, either to drown out the pain with food or as a desperate attempt to gain control over their body through deprivation. Drugs, alcoholism, or other addictive behaviors, including workaholism, may also be used to drown out the inner pain in both males and females. Suicidal ideation is an all too frequent result of sexual abuse as well. Females seem to make more suicide attempts, but males are more apt to succeed when they do try.

Another more subtle and hidden dynamic found when young children (before age 6 or 7) are sexually abused is dissociation. Dissociation is the opposite of association and refers to the compartmentalization of aspects of the function of the mind, including memory and feelings. In other words, the mind unconsciously separates what would normally be cohesively held together in a consistent perspective, sense of identity, and worldview.

In its extreme form, such dissociation can lead to Dissociative Identity Disorder (formerly called Multiple Personality Disorder). It has been estimated that 97% of those with Dissociative Identity Disorder (DID) have been severely abused, most of them sexually.[10] Many who have experience in this specialized field would estimate that approximately one to five percent of people in most local church bodies are struggling with these more complex dissociative issues.

Christians gifted with spiritual discernment who work in this field recognize that another consequence of sexual abuse is often demonization. Unfortunately, ungodly sex can be an avenue leading to this spiritual bondage. Understandably, then, the deterioration of Western culture in the past century has led to an explosion of demonization.

As is evident in the New Testament Gospels, a large part of Jesus' ministry involved delivering those who were "demon possessed." The Greek word used in these accounts is actually better transliterated as "demonized," as in modern English, "demon possession" implies a kind of ownership—which certainly could not be true of a Christian. Rather, the biblical term implies varying degrees of control and influence. Just as doctors can document that Christians can have cancer, those in deliverance ministries can document that Christians can be demonized, or held in bondage under influence of demons.

Important Considerations for Treatment

Understanding the effects and prevalence of child sexual abuse is important, but even more crucial is the need for the Christian community to provide more effective ministry to the large segment of our population who have been so abused. The last twenty years, in particular, have seen a substantial increase in secular research in regard to effective treatment modalities, which has documented and validated the work being done by a large number of Christian ministries that are now successfully addressing these issues as well. The approach for addressing child sexual abuse must be adjusted to the age of the person at the time intervention is started. If the abuse is discovered while the child is still pre-adolescent, it needs to be addressed by someone with training in "play therapy" and other modalities that take developmental issues into account and provide the necessary skills to meet the challenge of working with the child while avoiding suggestion. If the abuse is from outside the family, parental support becomes a vital and important part of the healing process. When one or both parents are involved in the abuse, however, children desperately need other safe adults who believe them and can provide a safe environment in which they can talk about their feelings. Competent help in healing must be provided by someone who knows the mandatory reporting laws for that particular state, while keeping the best interests and protection of the child clearly in mind.

It is also important to understand that often the need for a sexually abused child to deny that anything happened can be very strong, especially when a parent or primary caregiver is the perpetrator. When dissociation is involved, one part of the person may be very angry and disclose the abuse while another part may be very loyal to the perpetrator and deny, with all sincerity, that any abuse has taken place.

In too many cases, a child may dare to disclose the abuse, which leads to an inept investigation, followed by the child being severely punished by the perpetrators (sometimes in a way that leaves no outward sign of abuse) to reinforce the lesson that one must never talk about "family matters" to outsiders. This may be a major reason why many children never disclose their abuse in a way that brings lasting change to their abusive situation or why they recant an accusation they may have made. While false accusations are sometimes made, particularly in custody cases, it is important to remember that only five percent of sexual abuse perpetrators ever admit what they have done.

If the disclosure of abuse is made during adolescence, there is likewise a great need for someone to believe and support the teen. Although teens will have problems similar to those of younger children, the developing sexuality of adolescents usually adds to their shame and humiliation. Again, competent and well-trained help is needed to bring healing for the survivor, while being careful to follow all state-mandated reporting laws. Act wisely so that you do not put yourself (or your ministry) at legal risk.[11]

While not minimizing the complexity of the healing journey, the process of helping adults who reveal sexual abuse in their past is at least not complicated by state-mandated reporting laws. Although the adult may have greater emotional and spiritual maturity, their healing, nevertheless, is often made more difficult by a lifelong pattern of denying the reality of their abuse or minimizing it. For this reason, it is important that the survivor be in a safe environment and clearly understand that healing does not require accusation of alleged perpetrators (Rom. 12:18-19).

For Christians, the main goal is resolution of the psychological and spiritual dynamics resulting from the abuse, and ultimately, forgiveness of the perpetrator. Many Christians fail to understand that restoration of relationship with the perpetrator is a totally different matter (which is often not safe) and is not required for complete and thorough forgiveness to be given.

When the survivor is not in a safe environment, it is important to provide initial support without going too deeply into the trauma issues. Concentrate instead, on making their present environment safe and helping the person stay functional. It is also not wise to delve into painful memories until you ascertain that the person has sufficient ego strength, spiritual maturity, and community support to do so without being overwhelmed. Sometimes, developing a supportive relationship is most important initially in order to strengthen the person's capacity to complete the healing journey.

Uncovering an abusive past is similar to peeling away the layers of an onion. Peeling away too many layers too quickly can cause emotional instability, decreasing functionality, and in ex-

> **It is also important to keep in mind that demonization, when present, is a result of the problem, rather than the problem itself.**

treme cases, push a person toward suicide. It is critical that those providing help have an understanding of the many dynamics involved in these cases. This is especially important if the person demonstrates signs of demonization, dissociation, or DID.

Ministry to survivors of child sexual abuse is complex. Professional counsel is often needed since complications can be serious. A ministerial or prayer ministry approach can be effective with adequate training, however. Understanding mandated reporting laws is essential, as well as developing competent legal, medical and psychological support that can be accessed when needed. For those coming from a deliverance perspective, it is vital to be alert to the possibility of dissociation, which requires a more careful treatment approach. If deliverance is necessary, it should be done appropriately in a calm and gentle way that does not further traumatize the child or adult. One's authority does not depend on the volume of one's voice. Shouting or raising the voice can be traumatic to wounded survivors.

It is also important to keep in mind that demonization, when present, is a result of the problem, rather than the problem itself. If one can discover and remove the grounds claimed by spirits of darkness, they can be easily removed. Soul ties and sexual experiences outside of marriage are a frequent source of demonic attachments in these individuals, which need to be resolved. Other grounds include those passed down generationally—often involving covenants, oaths, and vows—as well as permissions given by caregivers. Grounds can also be given by rituals, ceremonies, or agreements made by the survivor. A more comprehensive list of grounds is available from materials on the Restoration in Christ Ministries website (www.rcm-usa.org).

The Healing Journey

No two people will experience healing in the same way. Age differences, severity of the abuse, age at onset, duration and coping skills used by the survivor will all affect the process of healing. There are, however, some common issues that need to be addressed for effective healing from child sexual abuse, whether dealing with a child, teen, or adult. Langberg has observed that, "the central experiences of childhood trauma are silence, isolation, and helplessness. Healing, then, must involve a restoration of voice, safe connection, and rightful power. Such healing cannot occur in isolation but rather must take place within the context of relationship."[12]

A major issue for all survivors is finding a way to identify and address the beliefs formed within the context of the abuse experience. Beliefs, such as, *it is my fault that it happened*, or *the abuse proves I am bad*, are common and may *feel* very true to the individual. These emotionally held beliefs are seldom changed using facts or logic. Rather, true healing usually comes when the person is emotionally in touch with the original event in which the belief/lie message was established and asking God to speak truth to that belief. This is a powerful method of bringing healing to the pain of sexual abuse, or any other issue held in place by a lie message.[13]

If treatment is started soon after the abuse, it is important to remember that a child is not developmentally capable of resolving all aspects of the abuse, nor is a teen. Each adult in treatment will have to be dealt with as an individual, adjusting treatment for their maturity level.

The good news is that even when child sexual abuse has left its trail of devastating effects, the person's life or usefulness to God does not end. Diane, with whom this chapter began, was a successful missionary and pastor's wife and has been in ministry with her husband for over 25 years. She now lectures internationally, telling her story and helping thousands of other survivors gain hope so essential for healing. She is a mature, joyous Christian with a servant heart whose life is very contagious and reflective of the Savior whom she loves very deeply. I should know—she is my wife. [14]

Notes

[1]   For a further description of such abuse, see Diane Mandt Langberg, Ph.D., *Counseling Survivors of Sexual Abuse* (Wheaton, IL: Tyndale House Publishers, Inc., 1997), pp. 61-62.

[2]   Judith A. Reisman, Ph.D, *Kinsey: Crimes & Consequences: The Red Queen & the Grand Scheme* (Arlington, VA: The Institute for Media Education, Inc., 1998).

3   David Middlebrook, *The Guardian System: S.T.O.P. Abuse Risk in Your Ministry* (Lake Mary, FL: Creation House [A part of Strang Communcations Company, www.creationhouse.com], 2000), p. 2.

4   Richard R. Hammar, Steven W. Klipowicz, and James F. Cobble, Jr., *Reducing the Risk of Child Sexual Abuse in Your Church: A complete and practical guidebook for prevention and risk reduction.* (Matthews, NC: Church Ministry Resources, 1993), p. 14.

5   Langberg, pp. 62-63.

6   Ibid., p. 66.

7   David Finkelhor, with Sharon Araji, Larry Baron, Angela Browne, Stefanie Doyle Peters, and Gail Elizabeth Wyatt, *A Sourcebook on Child Sexual Abuse* (Beverly Hills, CA: Sage Publications, 1986), p. 183.

8   Ibid., pp. 180-181.

9   Bessel A. van der Kolk, Alexander C. McFarlane, Lars Weisaeth. *Traumatic Stress: The Effects of Overwhelming Experience on Mind, Body and Society.* (New York, NY: The Guilford Press, 1996).

10   James G. Friesen, Ph.D., *Uncovering the Mystery of MPD* (San Bernardino, CA: Here's Life Publishers, Inc., 1991), p. 42.

11   For more information, see James Wilder, Ed. M. Smith. *Keeping Your Ministry Out of Court: Avoiding Unnecessary Litigation While Ministering to Emotionally Wounded People* (Campbellsville, KY: Alathia Publishing [www.care1.org], 2002).

12   Langberg, p. 61.

13   See Langberg. Also see Paula Sandford, *Healing Victims of Sexual Abuse* (Tulsa, OK: Victory House Publishers [www.Elijahhouse.org], 1988), and Diane Hawkins, *Multiple Identities: Understanding and Supporting the Severely Abused* (Grottoes, VA: Restoration in Christ Ministries [www.rcm-usa.org], 2002).

14   In addition to the resources noted above, I also recommend the following:
     •   Grant L. Martin, Ph.D., "Counseling for Family Violence and Abuse," *Resources for Christian Counseling*, General Editor, Gary R. Collins, Ph.D. (Waco, TX: Word Books, 1987).
     •   Frank W. Putnam, M.D., *Dissociation in Children and Adolescents: A Developmental Perspective* (New York, NY: The Guilford Press, 1997).
     •   William Sudduth, *So Free!!!: A Teaching on Deliverance.* (Pensacola, FL: Ram Inc. [www.ramministry.org], 2002).

Subject Index

John 8:11, 16
John 8:34,36, 23
John 8:44, 78
1 John 1:9, 39
1 John 2:16, 51
judgment(s), 66-67, 69-75

K
Keeping Your Ministry Out of Court, 104
1 Kings 11:7, 67
Kinsey, Alfred, 95
Kinsey: Crimes & Consequences, 103
Klipowicz, Steven W., 104

L
Lakeland Community Church
Langberg, Diane Mandt, 102, 103, 104
laws, reporting, 100
lesbian, 83-84
Leviticus 18:21, 65
Leviticus 18:22, 78
Leviticus 20:1-5, 65
Leviticus 20:13, 78
Lot, 66
lust, 13-14, 47-48, 56-58
lust, inherited, 17-18

M
Mark 16:9, 22
marriage, 25, 32-34, 36-37, 44, 45-46, 47, 60, 94, 96, 102
Martin, Grant L., 104
Mary Magdalene, 22
Mastering Life Ministries, 76

masturbation, 15, 16-17, 19, 48, 54
Matthew 2:18, 73-74
Matthew 5:6, 88
Matthew 5:27, 56
Matthew 5:28, 47
Middlebrook, David, 104
Ministering to Abortion's Aftermath, 64
mishkav zakur, 78
Molech, 65-73
mothers, spiritual, 54-61
Multiple Identities, 104

N
Noah, 13

P
Paul, 29, 30, 37, 55, 78
1 Peter 5:8,9, 48-49
2 Peter 1:3, 89
perversion, 47, 52
pornography, 14-16, 17, 47-48, 55-57, 59, 83
pornography, definition of, 14
poverty, spirit of, 70-71
prayer, 43-44, 60, 75, 90
pride, 39
prostitution, 17, 32
Proverbs 2:18, 30
Proverbs 5:22, 38
Proverbs 28:1, 73
Psalm 94:20-21, 66, 69
Psalm 106:36-42, 67

Look for other books in this series!

The Proven Foundations for Deliverance series continues with five other watershed books. Doris M. Wagner assembles top ministry practitioners to address specific topics of deliverance. Other books include:

Book One: Ministering Freedom from Demonic Oppression

Issues addressed include:
- The biblical basis for deliverance
- Can a Christian have a demon?
- Satan's plan to divert us from the path of God
- The believer's authority over demonic spirits
- How to minister spiritual housecleaning
- Deliverance in the local church
- How deliverance sustains revival

Book Two: Ministering Freedom to the Emotionally Wounded

Issues addressed include:
- Forgiving the unforgivable
- Releasing bitter root judgments
- Overcoming rejection
- Deliverance from fear and anger
- How trauma affects the whole person
- Mending cracks in the soul

For availability, please check your local Christian bookstore, call 877-924-6374, or visit www.wagnerpublications.org

Book Four: Ministering Freedom from the Occult   (Coming in Spring, 2004)

Issues addressed include:
- The occult and youth
- Witchcraft
- Curses and blessings
- Freemasonry, Voodoo, Santaria
- Ritualistic abuse in multiple personality disorder
- Common occult practices including New Age, hypnosis, certain martial arts, etc.

Book Four: Ministering Freedom to Family Issues   (Coming in Fall, 2004)

Issues addressed include:
- Ministering to childhood issues including adopted, unwanted, and wrong-sex children
- Abuses and addictions within the home
- Fatherlessness
- Divorce
- How to minister deliverance to a child
- Praying for teens
- Autism Spectrum Disorder and ADHD

Book Six: Practical Keys for Conducting a Deliverance Session   (Coming in Spring, 2005)

In this book, several seasoned deliverance practitioners will share effective methods and models for conducting a deliverance session.

(Please note: Titles, issues addressed, and release dates are subject to change.)